Organizational Science meets La

ROTTERDAM INSTITUTE OF LAW AND ECONOMICS

Erasmus Universiteit Rotterdam

Organizational Science meets Law and Economics

Klaus Heine

eleven international publishing

Published, sold and distributed by Eleven International Publishing
P.O. Box 85576
2508 CG The Hague
The Netherlands
Tel.: +31 70 33 070 33
Fax: +31 70 33 070 30
Website: www.elevenpub.com

Sold and distributed in USA and Canada
International Specialized Book Services
920 NE 58th Avenue, Suite 300
Portland, OR 97213-3786, USA
Tel: 1-800-944-6190 (toll-free)
Fax: +1 503 280-8832
orders@isbs.com
www.isbs.com

Eleven International Publishing is an imprint of Boom uitgevers Den Haag.

ISBN 978-90-8974-471-5

Printed in The Netherlands.

Table of Contents

Rector Magnificus, esteemed colleagues and friends,

1 Introduction

If one thinks of meetings usually one has a meeting in mind where friendly people come together who have similar interests, like each other's aptitude or may even belong to the same family. This type of meeting is friendly – although over time it may become somewhat boring to hear the same stories from the same people every time. In the opposite direction one may consider meetings where people's interests are totally different, one does not respect each other's morale and all is about converting the others to one's own beliefs. Those meetings are challenging, without doubt a sort of risky undertakings, often unpleasant, but sometimes also the beginning of friendship and productive initiatives.

However, there is a third category of meetings. This category is often neglected, which is no wonder if one considers this type of meeting in more detail. The participants know only little about each other and often they are also not very interested in getting to know something more about each other. If those meetings take place at all there is only little communication and participants tell each other only a few relevant things – which, besides, are often common knowledge. Afterwards those meetings are quickly forgotten. No one may even remember that a meeting had taken place. And, this seems to be the most relevant characteristic of such meetings, no one is unhappy to depart and to forget about the meeting. Back home everyone does business as usual. The third kind of meeting is very likely if the participants have a narrow *Weltanschauung*, are politicians with a strong vision of how to fix things or are members of academic schools which are very well established in the scientific community.

The third type of meeting also applies when one thinks of organizational science and law and economics. Both are very well established scientific disciplines, which are concerned with human behaviour on the individual and group level. Despite this similarity of the disciplines' subject both disciplines have not much to say to each other. There are some scholars who serve as a sort of interface between the disciplines,[1] but those scholars remain the exception to the rule.

1 Oliver Williamson (see e.g. 1975; 1985) is certainly one of these scholars. Also Richard Langlois, David Teece and Nicolai Foss may be counted among this rare species of scholars.

One may ask why organizational science and law and economics are only loosely coupled, if the disciplines' subject is overlapping so much. To answer this question one has to dig deeper and to look at the underlying paradigmatic assumptions of both disciplines. Even if the differences are somewhat overstated: while law and economics assumes rational individuals who maximize their individual utility, organizational science assumes bounded rational individuals who are (only) 'satisficers' (if such an individual has attained a certain level of utility, he or she is satisfied and stops activity, even if there are still unexploited opportunities). And to make the difference even more salient: while law and economics is clearly rooted in methodological individualism, organizational science is not so clear on that matter (Vanberg 1992). Also, diverse organizational approaches rooted in methodological collectivism exist.[2] This brings us to the last obvious difference between the two disciplines. Law and economics is a coherent approach, which explains human behaviour within the rational choice framework. Agents maximize individual utility within a set of (legal) constraints. Or, to keep it simple, there is only one approach of law and economics. Organizational science is different. It is not a coherent approach, but consists of different approaches, which try to explain human behaviour as well as organizational behaviour. Thereby the maximization of individual utility can be an explanation for human action, but other explanations are also seen as valid explanations for human behaviour. So, there is not one organizational approach, but organizational science consists of a whole bundle of more or less different approaches.

In the following the difficult relation between organizational science and law and economics will be in the epicentre of this contribution. Although it will turn out that there is no simple way to reconcile both disciplines, it should become clear that both disciplines can learn from each other. Especially contemporary law and economics could profit from a better integration of findings in organizational science, in order to tackle law and economics problems, where organizations are involved. To that aim in a first step a short review of the history of economic thought will be presented, which focuses on the question how organizational science departed from economics. Then, in a second step, it will be more analytically investigated why organizations have remained a black box for law and economics. Subsequently, two examples will be presented which highlight the need to reconcile insights from law and economics and organizational science, in order to

2 See e.g. Udehn (2002) and Felin & Foss (2005).

get a better understanding how formal institutions affect the behaviour of individuals inside of organizations. The first example will be concerned with 'incentive channelling' in case of 'incentive regulation' of energy firms, while the second example will be concerned with the question in which way the 'organizational design' of firms affects a proper compliance of individuals with liability rules.

Saying that law and economics and organizational science are apart, raises the question whether these two disciplines have ever had something in common, and if so, what triggered the parting.

A full account of all the reasons why law and economics and organizational science are not integrated within a general theory of human behaviour would fill a whole book. And even if that book would be written, a lot of questions would remain. Therefore, only fragments of the history of economic thought can be presented here. Nevertheless, the great lines of theory development should become clear.

If we start our review around the year 1900 we see neither a branch of social science research deliberately integrating law, economics and organizational issues, nor do we see fully developed and distinct branches of social science research, caring each for law, economics and organizational issues. What we see are glimpses of different social science paradigms, which are sometimes hosted by the same scholar. Vilfredo Pareto (1848-1923) might be recognized as such a person. He is one of the founding fathers of neoclassical welfare economics and one of the heroes of the marginal revolution in economics. Every student of economics knows the so-called Pareto criterion. The basic problem he addressed is that if we accept that value judgments are subjective and no cardinal comparisons of utility are possible, then it would be unscientific to evaluate individuals' utility against each other and to derive policy recommendations from that. The Pareto criterion provides a value-free solution to that problem. It simply says that if one person in society is made better off by a certain policy, and no one is made worse off, then social welfare can be increased. This criterion can be aligned with general equilibrium theory, which then constitutes neoclassical welfare economics. Welfare economics provides the basis for economists to judge whether market processes will automatically bring forth a social optimum or whether there is market failure and government has to impose regulations on the market. The crucial point is that welfare analysis takes place under a large set of very restrictive assumptions.[3] Pareto has contributed to the clearness and rigor of these assumptions. However, he may have felt the trade-off between rigor

3 A brilliant discussion of the rigorous assumptions of neoclassical welfare economics can be found in Kenneth Boulding's (1969) presidential address to the meeting of the American Economic Association in 1968, where he paraphrases the economics approach by suggesting an intellectual drama which might be subtitled "Snow White (the fairest of all) and the Seven Marginal Conditions".

and relevance when one is out for theory building in the social sciences. While at the beginning of his academic career he was mainly concerned with the fundamental and axiomatic issues of welfare economics, in his older years he was more occupied with the description and explanation of sociological issues. Besides other topics he was a pioneer in research about elites. For example, which characteristics does a person need in order to become a part of the elite? Or, which are the circumstances which lead to an elite's decline ('circulation of the elites')? This research is not as rigorous as his contributions to welfare economics, however it seems highly relevant to our understanding of a society's development and up to now it plays a role in organizational science (for an overview and application see, e.g., Nielsen 2007).

There are other scholars who, similar to Pareto, contributed to neoclassical economics and organizational science, as well as legal scholars who substantiated their legal arguments by insights from orthodox economics as well as from evolutionary science. For example, Judge Oliver Wendell Holmes (1841-1935) explained the legal development as an evolutionary process, but at the same time he incorporated insights from orthodox economics into his reasoning (Holmes 1897), which makes him one of the ancestors of law and economics.

Important is that at the beginning of the last century different social research paradigms can be identified. However, these paradigms were at their infant stage and sometimes researchers jumped between the different paradigms. This means that glimpses of contemporary law and economics and organizational science as distinct disciplines can be identified, but at that time they did not constitute different research programs.

The unfolding of economics (including law and economics as a subdiscipline) and organizational science as clearly different research programs in social sciences can be roughly dated to the time period between 1910 and 1950. Starting with economics, in this period neoclassical analysis penetrated nearly all fields of economic interest, like market structure, production, capital theory, public finance, distributional issues, money, business cycles, international trade, (Keynesian) macroeconomics et cetera. As a capstone of this period one may see Arrow's and Debreu's proof of existence of an equilibrium of a competitive economy (1954), which states rigorously that decentralized choices of an economy's agents will lead to a social optimum.

Between 1910 and 1950 economics became a science which is only concerned with the rational decision making of individuals. If firms became involved into economic reasoning, they were modelled as (technological) production functions, or, if they were involved in decision making, they were treated like single individuals. That is, neither organizational issues nor deviations from rational behaviour played a role in economics; the firm became a 'black box'.

Two publications may be mentioned which, at least indirectly, addressed organizational issues on the firm level: 1) Coase's seminal paper 'The Nature of the Firm' (1937), in which he claims that the boundaries of the firm are not (only) constituted by technological reasons, but by the amount of transaction costs. The idea is that in case transaction costs are lower when a good or service is performed within a firm hierarchy than when bought externally on the market, then that good or service *should* be performed within the boundaries of the firm. So, organizational structure plays an indirect role in Coase's approach, because a firm's organizational structure determines the level of transaction costs and subsequently make or buy decisions. 2) Berle and Means' book 'The Modern Corporation and Private Property' (1933) also addresses organizational issues indirectly. Berle and Means were the first who explicitly pointed to the informational asymmetry between management and shareholders. This informational asymmetry constitutes a severe principal-agent problem, because managers may try to exploit the uninformed owners of a firm. Although today these two publications are seen as important early contributions to an economic 'theory of the firm', at the time when they were published they only received little attention.

At the same time period, when the firm became a 'black box' in neoclassical economics, management issues – how to organize work effectively within a firm – became prominent. The trigger for that was certainly that modern mass production (think of the Ford T-Model) needed new forms of organizational design to become effective. Correspondingly business schools were founded or expanded, in order to train managers (e.g. the Dutch School of Higher Commercial Education in 1913 in Rotterdam or the Harvard Business School in 1908). Also, scholars with a practical background started with research programs that may be put under the heading of 'scientific management'. To name only a few of them: Frederick Taylor (1856-1915), Henri Fayol (1841-1925), Heinrich Nicklisch (1876-1946), Chester Barnard (1886-1961), Elton Mayo (1880-1949), or Fritz Nordsieck (1906-1984). These approaches were only loosely coupled, lacking a sort of paradigmatic umbrella. In the end all these approaches can be best qualified as a negative image of neoclassical economics in the sense that neoclassical economics is exclusively concerned with the investigation of market processes between firms, including the role of the price mechanism and industry structure, while scientific management is exclusively concerned with intra-firm issues.

Law and economics issues played neither a role in neoclassical economics nor in scientific management. Surely, legal aspects played a role in American institutionalism (e.g., Thorstein Veblen and John R. Commons), but at the beginning of the 1950ies this school of thought had lost its influence in economics, blamed to be unscientific, because of its focus on describing single cases and providing no general theory. However, in legal practice from time to time judges applied economic reasoning, in order to substantiate their decisions. For example, in 1947 Judge Learned Hand ruled in a famous torts case[4] that if the cost of preventing harm is equal or greater than the gravity of loss (C > GL) then the tortfeasor has met the due standard of care. Also in legal science from time to time economic reasoning was a spring of inspiration – however, more by accident than by purpose. In this regard a remarkable piece of work is Wertheim's unpublished dissertation 'Aansprakelijkheid voor schade buiten overeenkomst' (Extra-contractual liability for damage) from 1930 at the university of Leiden, in which he developed a theory of tort law very similar to the contemporary law and economics analysis of tort law (Kerkmeester 2003). However, those early treatments of law and economics were not concerned with organizational issues.

As of the beginning of the 1950ies economics had become a social science, which was clearly distinguishable from sociology, political science and scientific management. While the 1950ies were a time of consolidation for economics, for management science it was the time when the so-called 'behavioural theory of the firm' was created. This theory was aimed at shedding light into the 'black box' of the neoclassical firm (Day & Sunder 1996). Because in the next chapter the 'behavioural theory of the firm' will be analysed in more depth, at this moment it is sufficient to mention that it was the breakthrough for organizational science to becoming an independent branch of research within the theory of the firm. Moreover, the behavioural theory of the firm may be seen as the door opener for a multitude of other approaches in management science which are concerned with organizational issues, like neo-institutionalism (DiMaggio & Powell 1983, 1991), evolutionary (Nelson & Winter 1982) or postmodern approaches (Clegg 1990), only to name a few. Nowadays a multitude of different organizational theories exist, which only have in common that they deviate more or less

4 United States v. Carroll Towing Co. 159 F.2d 169 (2d. Cir. 1947).

from the neoclassical assumptions of rationality, utility maximization and methodological individualism.

As of the advent of the behavioural theory of the firm in the 1950ies and its establishment in the 1960 and 1970ies one can say that economics and organizational science have become separated research paradigms in social science. Surely, there may be some overlapping, but the differences between the two paradigms are pretty clear.

Then, in the 1960ies law and economics came into play as an approach for analyzing a society's formal legal rules by the help of the economics toolbox. In general, law and economics can be understood as part of a larger movement in economics, which aimed at crossing the border from the traditional fields of economic analysis to the neighbouring disciplines of political science, sociology and law as well as history. With the help of the broader focus of new institutional economics and law and economics it became possible for economics to have a look inside the 'black box' and to analyse the firm as a means of hierarchical co-ordination of productive activities.

However, the development of the modern economic theory of the firm was not only a by-product of economics crossing its borders. There are at least two additional reasons. The first one may be termed 'counterreaction'. In the 1960ies the behavioural theory of the firm became a successful means to explain firm behaviour beyond production functions. Even though the behavioural theory of the firm is not totally contradicting neoclassical economics, its basic assumptions of bounded rationality and satisficing, are at odds with neoclassical economics. So, neoclassical economics was challenged to provide a theory of the firm which could more realistically explain firm behaviour and which could also be integrated into general equilibrium theory. Or, to put it in a more Coasian style of phrasing: a theory was needed that understands firms as 'islands of conscious power' (1937), which are embedded in a market structure and which are interacting with each other through the price mechanism (Teece 1996). The second reason why law and economics became prominent in the theory of the firm is that the legal rules determining a traditional firm's governance structure can be explained by microeconomic arguments of bilateral exchange (Alchian & Demsetz 1972). In addition, traditionally the firm is seen as a static monolith with clear cut firm boundaries, a clear hierarchy and it is obvious who the firm's owners are (Teece 1996). In this case it is also relatively easy to decide who should control a firm by which means, in order to tackle informational asymmetries. Corporate law and other business laws apparently mirror those economic concerns (Chandler

1962). From this early view of law and economics, scholars got the impression that business law is the emergent result of relatively simple underlying economic regularities (Demsetz 1967) and that business law resembles economic wisdom which has been accumulated and incorporated over centuries into contemporary business law. And one may conclude from this that it must be – with today's economic knowledge – possible to optimally design business law. The invisible hand of law production may now be substituted by purposeful economic law design. For example, one might think of sophisticated corporate governance rules which can overcome diverse kinds of principal agent problems.

Here it is not possible to survey all facets of the law and economics approach of the theory of the firm, however, two features shall be highlighted, which characterize this approach fairly well: (1) The firm as a quasi-market (Jensen & Meckling 1976) and (2) the firm as a 'legal fiction' (Jensen & Meckling 1976, p. 311). By the term 'quasi-market' it is meant that a firm is an assembly of bilateral contracts. This 'nexus of contracts' (Fama & Jensen 1983, p. 302; Jensen & Meckling 1976) is organized by a central contractor (management), in order to save transaction costs and to realize economies of scale within a team-production (Alchian & Demsetz 1972). The firm as a nexus of contracts and quasi-market perfectly fits into the market logic of general equilibrium theory. Understanding the firm as a 'legal fiction' means that business law is a veil which overcoats the underlying economic bargaining processes within a firm. Thereby it is left open which part of the nexus of contracts is covered by which specific law. For example, in some countries corporate law may govern almost exclusively the internal relations of shareholders, while in other jurisdictions other issues, like co-determination or relations with creditors, are also regulated (Heine & Kerber 2002). That is, while the explanation of the firm remains universally from a law and economics perspective, the specific law may vary to a certain degree. The charm of this approach of the theory of the firm is apparent: there is a general economic theory of the firm, which simultaneously allows for quite different legal orders in reality.

Surely, since the 1970ies a lot of insights have been added to the theory of the firm from a law and economics perspective. For example, today there is new property rights theory (Grossman & Hart 1986), incomplete contracts theory (Hart & Moore 1988) or the literature on competition between corporate laws (Romano 1985, 1993; Heine & Kerber 2002), only to name a few. However, organizational design issues only play a role insofar as they can be translated into principal agent or incomplete contract terms. Organizational design issues become reduced to corporate governance issues.

It is important that law and economics has managed for a theory of the firm which is in no conflict with the basic assumptions of neoclassical economics on the one hand and which allows the break-up of the 'black box' by integrating it into the general equilibrium framework on the other hand. As a consequence the contemporary perspective of law and economics on firm issues makes no reference to organizational theories, which are beyond the neoclassical framework.

At this point one may ask whether organizational science has made a connection to law in general and law and economics in particular. In the last decades organizational science has established itself as a label of all kinds of theoretical approaches which explain organizational issues. These diverse approaches are more or less apart from the perspective of law and economics on firms (Santos & Eisenhardt 2005). What seems to be the key hindrance for organizational science to collaborate with legal scholars in general and law and economics scholars in particular is that organizational theories cannot easily be used to interpret and improve specific legal rules. The reason is that often organizational theories lack clear-cut functional relations between an organization's elements as well as between organizational design and performance. For example, culture may be the glue of an organization (Teece 1996), but in which way do an organization's members contribute to organizational culture exactly, how does culture emerge, how does it affect an organization's performance and how is it related to specific formal rules and to the whole legal order? This is not clear and depends strongly on an organizational theory's perspective.[5] Also, while the neoclassical theory of the firm is attached to the normative concept of economic efficiency, most organizational theories are only descriptive or belong to other normative concepts, like equity or legitimacy, which are not very exact concepts compared to economic efficiency. This makes it difficult for organizational scientists to communicate their ideas to legal scholars as well as for legal scholars to adopt those concepts for specific law improvements.

At the end of this chapter it can be stated that law and economics and organizational science are concerned with the same subject, the firm. Also, both approaches are concerned with the explanation of firm behaviour. However, besides these issues both approaches share little

5 From an economist's perspective, see especially Kreps (1996).

common ground, and the communication between law and economics and organizational science is rather limited.

In the following chapter it will be analysed in more detail why the firm remained a 'black box', even though law and economics contributed much to a better understanding of firms, and why up till now organizational science has failed to address legal issues of the firm.

3 Organization matters

The aim of legal rules is to constrain the behaviour of individuals. To put this statement a little bit different: law can be understood as a set of rules which sets incentives for agents to behave in a wanted way or to suppress unwanted behaviour. Thereby law can facilitate certain actions, like making it easy for trading partners to fix a mutual beneficial contract. Or, law can sanction behaviour, like declaring specific contractual clauses void, which obviously exploit a contractual partner.[6]

If one accepts in general that the main function of law is to set incentives for agents to behave in a certain predictable way, then one of the main tasks of legal science is the design of legal rules, which accomplish a rule maker's goals. For that reason law and economics is a powerful tool. However, it may be questioned whether the rationality assumption leads to a too narrow understanding of human nature (Jolls, Sunstein & Thaler 1998; Korobkin & Ulen 2000; Jolls 2007). And if that would be the case one may conclude that at least some legal designs will not yield the intended result. Individuals may behave in other ways than predicted by law and economics analysis. This concern shall become clearer by addressing some questions: (1) In which way become incentives diluted or amplified, if human behaviour is no longer seen as rational, but as bounded rational? (2) In which way is the effectiveness of incentives affected, if humans do not maximize utility, but show a sort of satisficing behaviour? (3) In which way are decisions affected, if not a single individual makes a decision but a committee or group of people? (4) In which way are incentives diluted or amplified, if incentives have to be channelled through an organizational structure to the decision-making agent? These are quite simple questions, but law and economics is in trouble to give conclusive answers, which is due to the rationality assumption on the one hand and the neglect of internal organization, which goes beyond a narrow understanding of corporate governance, on the other hand.

In recent years question one and two have received a growing attention in law and economics. A new subdiscipline has emerged, which is called behavioural law and economics (Jolls, Sunstein & Thaler 1998; Korobkin & Ulen 2000). Behavioural law and economics relaxes the rationality assumption of traditional law and economics and allows for a richer model of man (Faure 2009). All kinds of psychological effects,

6 An in-depth discussion of the role of law in society can be found in Kennedy (1985). He also discusses critically the role of law in the cosmos of economics.

like heuristics and biases (see, e.g., Kahneman, Slovic & Tversky 1982), are taken into account, in order to get a better understanding of human decision processes and to make better predictions of human behaviour (see the articles in Sunstein 2000). Through the lens of behavioural law and economics human decision-making processes become more complex and more realistic. But basic assumptions of behavioural law and economics remain the same as in traditional law and economics. The approach refers to methodological individualism and the normative base is welfare economics. That is, legal designs aim at setting incentives for individuals to meet the standard of welfare economics. Thereby the legal design takes into account that individuals behave in a non-rational way, which means that it can be in the interest of society as well as in the interest of individuals to be 'nudged' by legal institutions to make efficient choices (Thaler & Sunstein 2008). In summary, behavioural law and economics is in no conflict with welfare economics. However, it has paternalistic overtones ('nudging') which provoke some conflict with a liberal (and libertarian) mindset (Lobel & Amir 2008). So far behavioural law and economics is not concerned with organizational issues; questions three and four are left open.

In the following it will be examined why it is not easy to address questions three and four within the contemporary framework of law and economics. As it will turn out it needs great efforts to reconcile law and economics with organizational theory. However, it should become clear that it is worthwhile to enrich law and economics by insights of organizational theory in order to strengthen the explanatory power of law and economics as well as its ability to contribute to legal designs which improve social welfare.

In neoclassical economics the firm behaves as if it were an individual (Argote & Greve 2007). As mentioned earlier, what is going on inside the firm is hidden in a black box. The components of the black box are not known. But, what are the interactions between the individuals inside the firm? What is the relation between firm owners and firm members? Can the owner control, through contracts and other means, what the firm members do (Leibenstein 1979)? To answer these questions one has to know what is going on inside the firm.

It is possible to distinguish three basic lines of research, which are alternatives for a better understanding of firm behaviour and for integrating organizational issues into a theory of the firm: (1) complex objective functions, (2) new institutional economics of the firm, and (3) the behavioural theory of the firm.

3.1 Complex objective functions

The first alternative is to define 'complex objective functions'. This is an indirect way for including organizational structure as a decisive factor into law and economics reasoning. While usually it is assumed that a firm behaves like a single profit maximizing agent, this approach assumes that the management aims at other goals than profit maximization (Baumol 1959; Marris 1963; Williamson 1963). Management may be more interested in the maximization of sales, firm growth or spending money for lavish offices, extra secretarial services, luxury cars et cetera. The important point is that management becomes identified as a distinct organizational layer of the firm, which behaves not in the interest of shareholders. Then the firm consists of at least two organizationally distinct groups: the firm owners and the management. This separation makes it possible to construct complex objective functions of firm behaviour, which go beyond simple profit maximization. For example, one may put sales, growth rate, profit and managerial amenities as weighted variables in an objective function of management, with which then firm behaviour may be predicted. Also, psychological factors may become arguments of that objective function; for example, management may use certain routines and heuristics to achieve its goals instead of maximizing utility in each single case.

Law and economics analysis can be easily connected to this kind of research strategy by considering legal rules which target specific arguments in the objective function. But despite its seemingly great intuition one can question whether the approach of complex objective functions really solves the problem of aligning organizational issues with law and economics. The rationale for this is that the approach of complex objective functions, similarly to the black box view of the firm, assumes a single decision maker. Now the single decision-making agent is the management to whom a complex objective function is ascribed. That is, only the assertion about the behaviour of the black box has changed (Leibenstein 1979).

The essence of the organizational problem is not touched by the approach of complex objective functions. If there is only one manager who is maximizing his or her complex utility function, than no problem exists. But what meaning can be given to a situation where a group (of managers) makes a decision? Different managers may have different aims and may weigh the arguments of the complex objective function differently. How do the different utility functions of the managers become aggregated? It can be assumed that the larger the management group is and the greater the number of arguments in the complex objective function are that the greater the problem (Leibenstein 1979).

The approach of complex objective functions is silent on the meaning of group size and differences in power of group members. The approach is lacking an understanding of hierarchical conflict resolution mechanisms. Thereby it can be assumed that not only formal power relations shape group decisions, but also informal relations between group members influence group decisions (Salancik & Pfeffer 1977; Leibenstein 1979; French & Raven 1959). In the end it is dubious whether a complex objective function can accurately mirror group decisions and the organizational behaviour of firms. As a consequence it is also doubtful that legal rules which are aimed at arguments of a complex objective function are smart enough to adequately change organizational behaviour. What is lacking is a better understanding of the internal operations of a firm, which subsequently can be linked to a firm's legal framework.

3.2 NEW INSTITUTIONAL ECONOMICS OF THE FIRM

The second alternative to get more insight into the organizational behaviour of firms is the approach of new institutional economics, which is widely adopted by contemporary law and economics.[7] In the foregoing section this approach has already been discussed. The apparent feature of this approach is that organizational issues become decomposed in a nexus of bilateral contracts. Compared to the approach of complex objective functions this approach has no aggregation problem, because it looks at single contractual relations between firm members. That is, the firm as a black box is replaced by a nexus of contractual relations which is integrated into the general equilibrium of the market economy (Jensen & Meckling 1976; Fama & Jensen 1983). The consequence of this approach is that firms and other organizations have to be understood as legal fictions. What makes an organization different from a market transaction becomes blurred, or even arbitrary. Nevertheless, this approach allows gaining important insights into the black box by shedding light on specific contractual relations between members of a firm. In addition, law can be relatively easily targeted on these relations, in order to influence behaviour of agents and to improve social welfare.

7 For an overview of the approach of new institutional economics see Furubotn and Richter (2005).

Despite its ability to open the black box, the approach of new institutional economics fails to address important features of organizations, which cannot be translated into the category of voluntary exchange between equal trading partners. The point is that organization goes beyond matters which can be included into contracts and can be translated into an agency problem (Rajan & Zingales 1998, 2000). This statement needs some clarification.

Coase (1937, quoting Robertson 1923, p. 85) speaks of firms as 'islands of conscious power in this ocean of unconscious co-operation'. For him, firms are entities in which hierarchical power relations are means of co-ordinating productive activities, thereby contrasting voluntary exchange relations on markets. However, Coase did not clarify what he meant exactly by 'power' and 'hierarchy'. Only thirty five years later Alchian and Demsetz (1972) came back to the meaning of power in a firm. By integrating the firm into the equilibrium idea of a market economy they concluded that firm hierarchy is a monitoring device for the organization of teamwork. The idea is that in order to profit from the synergies of teamwork, all workers would freely agree to be monitored by management. In a famous passage they write: 'It is common to see the firm characterized by the power to settle issues by fiat, by authority, or by disciplinary action superior to that available in the conventional market. This is delusion. The firm does not own all its inputs. It has no power of fiat, no authority, no disciplinary action any different in the slightest degree from ordinary market contracting between any two people. I can "punish" you only by withholding future business or by seeking redress in the courts for any failure to honor our exchange agreement. That is exactly all that any employer can do. He can fire or sue, just as I can fire my grocer by stopping purchases from him or sue him for delivering faulty products.' (Alchian & Demsetz 1972, p. 777)

However, one may ask whether an employment relation is indeed equal to buying a product at a store. This has been forcefully questioned by Grossman, Hart and Moore, which have developed the so-called new property rights theory (Grossman & Hart 1986; Moore 1992). This theory states that power is a means to foster and to protect relationship-specific investments in an environment where contracts are incomplete. Power is then a mechanism to exercise rights which are not contractible (Rajan & Zingales 1998). Moore (1992, p. 497) explains: 'When a customer "fires" Alchian and Demsetz's grocer, the grocer (being a separate contractor) gets to keep the store; whereas if the grocer were an employee of the customer, the customer (the boss) could deny the grocer (the worker) access to the store, and could hire another grocer on the spot labor market.' That is, a firm owns the residual right to keep the worker off the firm, while the worker has no equal property right.

Residual rights are vested by ownership. An owner of an asset can determine how it should be used and who is entitled to use it. In case of disputes the owner can refuse the use of the asset. Hence, the core definition of the firm is not based on contracts but on the ownership of physical assets. From that, one can ask which allocation of property rights is the most efficient one. The aim is to allocate residual rights of control in a way that, in case of incomplete contracts, the discretionary power of ownership fills the contractual gap. Thereby the allocation of property rights shall make relationship-specific investments feasible. It is apparent that the approach of new property rights theory has an understanding of power in a theory of the firm, which is lacking in the contractual theory of the firm (Rajan & Zingales 1998). It is also obvious that law is the instrument with which residual rights of control are designed and allocated, in order to shape the power structure of firms. With the explicit recognition of power as an important component of firm hierarchy the new property rights theory has made a step forward, in order to integrate an essential category of organizational science into law and economics thinking. However, in total the integration of organizational issues is very limited. The reason is that new property rights theory is only concerned with the ownership of physical assets (Rajan & Zingales 1998), but ownership of physical assets is not the only source of power in an organization. There are other sources of power, which might be more effective for promoting relationship-specific investments.

Employees undoubtedly belong to an organization and without employees an organization is difficult to imagine. An organization's economic success crucially depends on the relationship-specific human capital of employees. However, new property rights theory does not conceive employees as part of the firm. Because employees cannot be owned, they are no part of the firm; they are not treated differently from agents with which the firm deals at arm's length (Rajan & Zingales 1998). Other power relations, like co-specialization of employees with firm assets and the design of an organizational architecture, which grants smart access rights to a firm's critical assets (like intellectual property rights), are not considered (Stieglitz & Heine 2007).

In summary the new institutional economics approach of the firm has to be evaluated in a balanced way. On the one hand it allows looking inside the black box, on the other hand internal organization plays only a minor role in this approach. While in the contractual view of the firm hierarchical power relations are defined away and the firm becomes a quasi-market of bilateral contracts, in the property rights view of the firm power is reduced to a means of closing contractual gaps. Even though new property rights theory identifies power as an important means for the organization of firms, the theory does not include employees as core components of firms, because employees cannot be owned (Rajan & Zingales 1998, 2000). Another drawback of the contractual as well as the property rights view of the firm is that agents are assumed as rational, which makes it conceptually difficult where informal organizational structure comes into play. For example, organizational culture is neglected, which is the heart of an organization's informal structure. Organizational culture is 'the pattern of beliefs and expectations shared by the organization's members. These beliefs and expectations produce norms that powerfully shape the behavior of individuals and groups.' (Schwartz & Davis 1981, p. 33) If the role of informal rules is neglected, then a big part of the organizational problem is omitted (Teece 1996). It also becomes questionable whether the theory has embraced enough of the reality, in order to make valid statements (see, e.g., the empirical study by Simester & Wernerfelt 2005). Therefore it is open to the future whether the new institutional economics approach of the firm can be amended in a way which allows embracing organizational issues which go beyond a narrow understanding of corporate governance (Santos & Eisenhardt 2005).

3.3 The behavioural theory of the firm

The third alternative for getting a better understanding of what is going on inside the black box is the behavioural theory of the firm. It has been developed since the 1950ies mainly at Carnegie Mellon University in Pittsburgh by scholars like Simon, Cyert and March. The Carnegie school understands itself as giving a 'body to the black box of the neoclassical firm in the form of empirically relevant, process-oriented models of concrete decisions in organizations.' (Day & Sunder 1996, p. 139) Yet, the behavioural theory of the firm is concerned with the analysis of a variety of intra-organizational problems (for an overview see Argote & Greve 2007) and it is more a set of ideas than a coherent theory (Leibenstein 1979; Levinthal 2005).

Since the behavioural theory of the firm is not yet a theory in a strict sense, it is not possible to identify a core model from which the theory's assertions can be deduced. But it is possible to identify ten basic characteristics of the approach (Day 1964; Leibenstein 1979). These are: (1) satisficing, (2) bounded rationality, (3) multiplicity of goals, (4) sequential attention to goals, (5) feedback, (6) standard operating procedures, (7) resistance to change except under 'duress', (8) coalitions to resolve conflicts, (9) organizational slack to stabilize coalitions, and (10) maintenance of viability. All ten characteristics imply a departure from neoclassical economics as well as from the view of new institutional economics on firms. Satisficing, bounded rationality and sequential attention to goals are concerned with the human incapability of performing maximizing behaviour. Feedback and standard operating procedures may be understood as the use of organizational routines, in order to cope with incomplete knowledge as well as to incorporate past experience into current decision-making processes. Resistance to change except under 'duress', coalitions to resolve conflicts, organizational slack to stabilize coalitions and maintenance of viability have to be understood as the need to implement hierarchical organizational structures and other organizational mechanisms, which allow for timely firm decisions without running the risk that internal conflicts lead to a firm's unwinding.

These ideas can be condensed to four major research fields of the behavioural theory of the firm (Augier 2004). The first is the quasi-resolution of conflict. Avoiding conflict involves factoring problems into subproblems and delegating authority to solve the subproblems. The second field of research is uncertainty avoidance (risk aversion). Firms try to avoid uncertainty by delaying decisions until the uncertainty is resolved through the unfolding of events, and by negotiating the internal and external environment through budgets and contracts. The third research field is concerned with so-called problemistic search. Search processes are assumed to be motivated by problems, simple-minded in its causal models, and biased by goals and experiences. The fourth research field is organizational learning. Firms adapt their aspiration levels according to their experience and the experience of others. Because different parts of an organization see different things and evaluate things differently, different parts of the organization learn different things from past experiences.

These ideas have inspired a large number of organizational theories (for an overview see Argote & Greve 2007). For example, neo-institutionalism explains how firms adapt to a symbolic environment of cognitions and expectations as well as to the regulatory environment of rules and sanctions (DiMaggio & Powell 1983). Thereby neo-institutionalism assumes bounded rationality, uncertainty avoidance and decision making under ambiguity (Meyer & Rowan 1977; DiMaggio & Powell 1983). As a result of this borrowing from the behavioural theory of the firm, some branches of neo-institutionalism, such as the research field on the diffusion of institutions (for a review see Strang & Soule 1998), come to predictions which are quite similar to those of the behavioural theory of the firm (see, e.g., Levitt & March 1988; Greve 1996).

Although it is not possible to give here a full account of the behavioural theory of the firm and all the subsequent organizational theories which have been inspired by it, it should become clear that the behavioural theory of the firm is a vehicle to get more insight into the internal operations of organizations. In particular, organizational hierarchies become of major interest, because hierarchy is the means with which conflicts are resolved, information is transmitted and with which organizational learning is spurred or blocked.

While in the approach of complex objective functions and the new institutional economics of the firm the meaning of internal organization is underexposed, it is the dominant research objective in the behavioural theory of the firm. However, the consequence of the nearly exclusive focus on internal organization is that questions about the way external regulations affect firm behaviour take a back seat in the behavioural theory of the firm. As a consequence, the behavioural theory of the firm has missed the chance to become a cornerstone for the law and economics analysis of the firm.

But there are also other reasons why the behavioural theory of the firm has so far only contributed a little to the law and economics analysis of firms. A simple but powerful explanation is that organizational science scholars are seldom interested in legal matters, nor are they trained in legal issues. In other words, the profession of organizational science only seldom crosses the border to the legal sphere and vice versa. In addition, there are also methodological reasons why law and economics has difficulties to adopt insights of the behavioural theory of the firm. The main point is that the setting of legal rules implies that there is some consensus about the quality of the problem and the underlying causal mechanisms which shall be regulated by law. Law cannot be applied on an ad hoc basis, but has to be stable and equally applied (rule of law) to a large number of cases (Scalia 1989). This implies that a law maker can only refer to a theory with a core of basic assumptions and mechanisms which fit to all subjects and cases under scrutiny. That is, a theory of the firm must claim to be applicable to all kinds of firm issues which are relevant to explaining the existence and functioning of firms. A theory of the firm which is not generalizable has only little value for law making, and the behavioural theory of the firm obviously has a problem with generalization.

In a revealing passage Cohen and Cyert (1975, p. 51) state that on the industry (or aggregate) level the neoclassical approach seems to be appropriate, while for predicting specific firm behaviour it is recommended to refer to the behavioural theory of the firm. 'At this level of generality, we think that the results deduced from a set of assumptions which include utility and profit maximization are perfectly acceptable. If we wish to predict how a particular household or firm will behave, then assumptions this general will not be satisfactory.' Apparently, there is a methodological problem. If neoclassical theory cannot predict single firm behaviour, how can it predict firm behaviour on the industry level? Or, if a theory can predict single firm behaviour, why can it not predict aggregate behaviour (Leibenstein 1979)? An answer is still pending.

An explanation for the methodological problems may be derived if one looks on the research strategy of the behavioural theory of the firm. While the neoclassical and new institutional economics theories of the firm assume *a priori* a specific behaviour of firms, the behavioural theory of the firm criticizes this apriorism by pointing to the neglect of internal organization and empirical validity of those theories (Verma & Churchman 1997). Cyert (1988, p. xv) puts the research strategy of the behavioural theory of the firm in the way that it should contribute toward 'making micro economics an empirical science rather than a deductive one.' This inductive research strategy has led to the situation that the behavioural theory of the firm has assembled a lot of important findings about the internal organization of firms. However, these findings have not yet merged into a general behavioural theory of the firm, from which it is possible to draw straightforward conclusions for law design. For example, the behavioural theory of the firm understands firms as coalitions of individuals, whereby individuals may have different goals (Cyert & March 1959). The empirical question is then, how organizations come to a decision, if the goals of organizational members differ. It is also a question how a coalition becomes stabilized, if the individual goals are different. These are surely important research questions for a theory of coalitions. However, a theory of coalitions is not presented. It is not exactly stated how coalitions are formed, who gets into a coalition, or who receives which benefits. It is simply assumed that the firm is a coalition and then the subsequent problems become scrutinized. Nevertheless, the theory has the aspiration to provide a conclusive theory of coalitions (Leibenstein 1979). However, reviewing the literature draws the picture that a core model of coalition has still to be awaited and that Cyert's and March's programmatic outlook from 1959 (p. 89) is still relevant: 'Before the theory can develop further, however, and particularly before it can focus intensively on the formation of objectives through bargaining and coalition formation (rather than on the revision of such objectives and the selective attention to them), we require greater empirical clarification of the phenomena involved.'

In summary, the behavioural theory of the firm addresses a lot of important questions related to a better understanding of the internal organization of firms, which are highly relevant if one is out to incentivize a particular firm behaviour by the help of legal instruments. For example, in which way will an external regulation be channelled through the firm's hierarchical organization to the decision-making agent, or in which way will a firm's organization generate and transmit the relevant information which is needed to make a proper decision in accordance with the law maker's goals?

However, the lack of a core model which allows deriving hypotheses on the way organizational structure affects firm behaviour, makes it complicated to use the behavioural theory of the firm as an instrument for law making and legal improvement. This especially becomes clear when the behavioural theory of the firm is compared to the new institutional economics theory of the firm. The new institutional economics theory of the firm not only provides a theoretical core for the understanding of firm behaviour, but also uses the categories of 'contract' and 'property rights', which makes it easy to link this approach to legal thinking. In addition, new institutional economics fits into the normative concept of welfare economics, while the behavioural theory of the firm is either silent on this or is not clear on how to aggregate single firm behaviour on the market level. But a normative benchmark is indispensable if one is out to make legal recommendations.

On the other hand, new institutional economics widely ignores internal organization, which goes beyond the contractual framework and principal agent relations.[8] This makes it doubtful that new institutional economics can embrace enough of today's real world firm phenomena, like firm networks which have no clear firm boundary and for which

8 For an important challenge of the traditional principal agent approach see also the contributions by Blair and Stout (1999; 2001a, b) who consider the firm as a complex team production, in which a corporation's directors are seen as fiduciaries of all stakeholders. For an overview of this approach see Lan and Heracleous (2010).

no distinct legal form is available (Rajan & Zingales 1998; 2000; 2001; Zingales 2000; Davis & Marquis 2005). A related problem is that the new institutional economics theory of the firm might be a rigorous theory, but it might not be able to solve relevant empirical problems and to inform law makers how to tackle contemporary problems of firm organization (Zingales 2000; Rajan & Zingales 2000). For example, antitrust may detect the abuse of vertical market power by a single firm. However, the firm might not exert abusive power, but is actually co-ordinating a network of activities within a firm boundary that antitrust cannot identify, because it relies on the legal firm boundaries, not the economic ones determined by organizational necessities (Zingales 2000; Santos & Eisenhardt 2005).

4 A way out of the dilemma?

So far it has become clear that law and economics and organizational science are branches of social science research, which are relatively isolated from each other. Nevertheless, one has the feeling that not only both disciplines might learn a lot from each other, but that an integrated approach would yield a high level of explanatory power as well as could inform law makers how to improve firm law. But a sort of theory integration is not within sight. The paradigmatic differences between the deductive approach of law and economics and the inductive research program of the behavioural theory of the firm are too different that there could be an easy reconciliation and merger into one integrated theory of the firm. One has to speculate whether in the future there will be integration at all and in which way this integration may come about.

If there will be an integrated theory it is very likely that it will be triggered by new institutional economics. The reason for this conjecture is that the new institutional economics theory of the firm is a relatively solid theory building, which is centred around the categories of contracts and property rights. This makes it possible to gradually implement and amend insights from organizational science to that body of literature. In contrast, organizational science is a highly dispersed body of literature. The fragmentation of organizational science makes it difficult to connect insights from new institutional economics to it in a systematic way, and ultimately one cannot expect theory integration which is triggered by organizational science.

An interesting example of an extended view of new institutional economics, which is informed by organizational science, is the approach by Rajan and Zingales (1998; 2000; 2001). They amend the new property rights framework in a way which makes it possible to conceive employees as a strategic resource, which is not only contractually bound to the firm, but also through its ownership of relationship-specific knowledge. That is, while the shareholders have (legal) power to grant or to deny employees the access to a firm's specific assets (physical and intellectual property), the employees can co-specialize to these assets, making the use of physical and intellectual property only then profitable. In this way employees become dedicated to the firm's assets. On the one hand, this makes the employees vulnerable, because they cannot use their specific knowledge outside the firm. On the other hand, they get power, because as a co-specialized resource they cannot be easily replaced by the firm's shareholders.

From this framework Rajan and Zingales derive requirements for an efficient internal organizational structure of the firm, which protects a firm's idiosyncratic resources (Stieglitz & Heine 2007). Rajan and Zingales show also that the economic and the legal definition of the firm can fall apart and that the enforcement of certain legal forms for doing business as well as regulations may cause economic inefficiencies. The future will decide whether this approach is powerful enough to serve as a solid theoretical base for the alignment of law and economics and organizational science.

However, even without an integrated theory it is possible to benefit from both worlds – the rigor of law and economics and the relevance of organizational science. The idea is that normatively the benchmark of welfare economics remains effective. This assures that there is a clear and identifiable benchmark in place with which the effectiveness of different legal options can be evaluated. On the positive level insights from organizational science shall be used, in order to get a better understanding of the way in which law affects organizational behaviour.[9] The idea is that insights of organizational science make it possible to develop smart laws and regulations, which have a high(er) probability to achieve the law maker's goals. Surely, this approach draws the same criticism as behavioural law and economics: the paternalistic notion on the normative level and the eclecticism on the positive level (Lobel & Amir 2008 for a discussion see Arcuri 2008). But as long as there is no integrated theory available, it seems pragmatic to take this way and to leave it to the empirical test, which approach can reach the law maker's goals most effectively.

In the remainder of this contribution two examples will be sketched out, which give an impression of how insights from organizational science can be connected to law and economics and regulation. The first example is concerned with 'incentive channelling' on energy markets. It shall become clear that the firm is not an individual, but a collective actor, and that an incentive for the firm is not necessarily an incentive for a decision maker inside the firm. Thus the success of regulation depends on the channelling of incentives through the organization to the decision-making agent. As it turns out, neglecting the relevance of organizational issues for targeting regulatory incentives results in poor regulatory outcomes. The second example points to the relevance of or-

9 In behavioural law and economics on the individual level we find the same approach. On the normative level the principles of welfare economics prevail, while on the positive level a richer model of human behaviour is employed (see, e.g., Thaler & Sunstein 2008).

ganizational structure for making better informed group decisions. By the example of tort liability it will be shown that the probability of making harmful decisions as well as selling defective products depends on the employed organizational structure. This means, by implication, that a firm may be held liable if it has not installed an organizational structure which can properly evaluate risks. Both examples open the gate to a lot of subsequent questions for law and economics research. Of course only some of these questions can be addressed here.

5 The relevance of organization for law and regulation

5.1 Incentive channelling on energy markets – the interplay between external regulation and organization[10]

5.1.1 *Setting up the problem*

In ordinary markets, competition is an automatic incentive device that makes sure that in the long run only those firms will prevail that can offer products at a competitive price level. However, energy markets are different. They are characterized by the market structure of natural monopoly. While in ordinary markets production functions have decreasing returns to scale, firms in energy markets operate with a production function of increasing returns to scale. This is largely because of the power grid, from which result network externalities and which makes it reasonable to run only one single grid infrastructure. The crucial point is that natural monopoly constitutes market failure (Viscusi, Harrington & Vernon 2005) and market selection is interrupted.

From a normative point of view, the structurally hampered market process affords regulatory intervention, in order to constrain the uncontrolled exercise of monopoly power. Therefore, in the past, the energy sector was heavily regulated by jurisdictions. The traditional regulation schemes were intended to overcome the problem of natural monopoly and to implement second-best solutions. However, over the years, it became clear that the traditional method of regulating energy markets did not function well. Energy prices remained high in comparison to the prices indicated for other markets (Goerten & Clement 2006; Eurostat 2006), the investment in new technologies was low or arbitrary, and customer service was bureaucratic (Mikkelsen, Nybo & Gronhaug 2002). Therefore, since the 1980ies, a growing number of jurisdictions have tried to overcome these undesirable results by implementing new kinds of regulation.

All these new regulatory policies have in common the fact that they aim to establish (a) external incentives for energy firms to become more efficient (incentive regulation of the power grid) and (b) question the level of vertical integration of energy firms (unbundling of the power grid from production and selling of energy).

10 For a more detailed discussion see Heine (2011).

a) Incentive regulation aims to mimic market incentives. The idea is that managers of grid firms should be stimulated to use their superior knowledge about cost reductions for making the distribution of energy more efficient (for an overview see Vogelsang 2002; Laffont 1994). In order to achieve this aim, incentive regulation makes a paradigmatic shift: instead of regulating the costs of the net-infrastructure directly (so-called cost-plus regulation), it specifies a 'price cap' (Acton & Vogelsang 1989; Littlechild 1983; Shleifer 1985). A 'price cap' is the highest possible price that the owner of the power grid can charge in exchange for granting access to the grid for energy producers. If the owner of the power grid can manage to reduce costs below the ceiling of the 'price cap', he can keep the difference as an extra profit. It is obvious that managers of grid firms should have a strong incentive to reduce costs in order to gain that extra profit.
b) There are two ways for separating the power grid from the production and sale of energy: (1) the governance mode of 'legal unbundling' and (2) the governance mode of 'ownership unbundling'. In case of legal unbundling, the power grid is the property of an energy firm that is also engaged in the production and sale of energy. However, under a legal unbundling regime, the power grid firm has to be an independent legal entity (for example, a public limited company or private limited company). It has the obligation to grant non-discriminatory access to the grid for all competitors in energy markets and to serve as a 'common carrier'. In the case of ownership unbundling, the grid firm becomes totally separated from the production and sale of energy. The owners of the grid firm must not be engaged in the production and sale of energy. Because the only operation of the grid firm is the distribution of energy, it can be expected that the grid firm will grant equal access to the grid for all producers of energy, in order to maximize profits from the brokerage of grid capacities.

Thus, the effectiveness of regulation does not solely depend on the employed incentive scheme but also depends on the access to the power grid and the vertical organization of energy supply. This makes it intuitively clear that organizational questions become highly relevant, as one has to ask in which way incentive regulation interacts with the various parts of the supply chain. Until now, however, the interaction of incentive schemes with the vertical organization of energy firms has not received much attention (Joskow 1991; 2006).

An obvious question is, for example, to what extent the effectiveness of incentive regulation depends on the legal form of unbundling.

As yet, models of incentive regulation are silent on this point. Their focus is exclusively on the impact of external regulations on grid firm behaviour, whereby it is implicitly assumed that the grid firm behaves like a single individual and that there are no countervailing effects from a grid firm's organization. It is largely ignored that organizational structure represents a set of 'internal regulations' to decision makers. Additionally, models of incentive regulation assume that all agents behave rationally. However, this assumption may be too narrow for the analysis, given that managers are bound to 'external' as well as to 'internal' regulations, which both may produce contradictory incentives, which are cognitively not easy to reconcile.

5.1.2 *Transaction cost economics as a link between external regulation and organization*

A starting point for getting more insight into the complex interplay between external regulation and organizational issues and to narrow down the problem of incentive channelling is transaction cost economics. Transaction cost economics qualifies as a bridge between regulation and firm behaviour (Williamson 1996).

Transaction cost economics analyses different modes of co-ordination that range between markets and hierarchies, thereby appreciating bounded rationality of agents and culture as important theoretical building blocks (for an overview, see Williamson 1998). In the epicentre of transaction cost economics is the 'transaction', which may be broadly understood as every kind of exchange between two or more agents. Transactions are a part of all kinds of contracts or binding arrangements, including purchase contracts, employment contracts, corporate law or regulations. Those contracts belong in turn to the entire institutional environment, which might be comprised of the judicial system, the political system or the set of informal rules mediated by culture (for an overview see Nee 2005). In addition, transactions depend on the technological specifics of goods and services – for example, whether a transaction demands sunk investments or not (Williamson 1998). In any event, transactions produce costs, and the question is which governance mode minimizes those costs. That is, whenever a transaction via the market mechanism fails, then hierarchical co-ordination may be in order because hierarchical co-ordination may save transaction costs (Williamson 1998).

In case of energy firms, one has to determine the governance mode that minimizes the transaction costs of co-ordinating the energy supply chain. A hierarchical co-ordination of activities is given, if there is a bundling of production, distribution and sale of energy in a legal entity, which serves as a parent company (e.g. a management holding) making all strategic decisions along the value chain. It can be argued that this governance mode is the most transaction cost-saving for energy firms because there are significant sunk costs associated with the power grid and substantial expenditures related to its technical operation, as well as the co-ordination between the production of energy and its transmission via the grid (Joskow 2006). More generally, the exploitation of synergies and complementarities between the production, distribution and sale of energy calls for integrated hierarchical co-ordination (Stieglitz & Heine 2007).

But, putting the energy supply chain under the control of integrated management raises a dilemma. On the one hand, integrated management may reduce transaction costs, bring forward synergies and enhance productivity. On the other hand, the power grid is a natural monopoly that may be abused to leverage monopoly power from the distribution of energy toward the production and sale of energy. For example, an integrated energy firm may impede access to the grid for competitors by giving priority to its own operations and run short the capacity of the grid. In effect, reducing the capacity of the grid retains monopoly profits and causes welfare losses.

It is apparent that transaction cost economics seemingly has a lot to contribute to the understanding of the interrelation between organizational structure and the regulation of energy firms, as well as to the appropriate design of corporate governance and regulations of the energy sector. Amazingly enough, public policy has remained, by and large, unaffected by the insights of transaction cost economics. This appraisal has been underpinned by Joskow (1991, p. 77): 'However, while transaction cost economics has played a role in the debates about vertical restructuring in these industries, and the precise form that such restructuring should take, it is my sense that the direct role of transaction cost considerations in influencing the direction of public policy has, so far, been quite modest.' Even though this statement is twenty years old, it is still relevant.

5.1.3 Transmission failures of market incentives into transaction cost minimal organizational structures

In order to analyse the behaviour of agents in energy firms in more detail, one can ask whether the processing of external incentives through the organization of regulated firms is different from that of firms in unregulated markets.

Under the conditions of workable competition, market forces select firms (Alchian 1950). Thereby incentives are processed from the consumers' product choices via the corporate veil to the decision-making agents. These market-driven incentives are high-powered and lead to an adaptation of more effective organizational structures by firms (Cooter & Ulen 2008, pp. 143). As a result, firms experiment with new organizational forms which support the channelling of incentives. That is, the decentralized discovery procedure of competition (Hayek 2002) automatically reveals which firms have the best organizational structure, in order to tackle the problem of incentive channelling (Kole & Lehn 1997, 1999; for a recent survey of the literature see Love 2010).

In regulated markets, there is no such automatism. Instead, the regulator artificially forms the selection environment by granting monopoly and simultaneously regulating prices and quality. The crucial point is that consumers cannot freely choose between different products and services but have to take the offers that have been pre-specified by the regulator. This implies an important consequence: while in ordinary markets, firms have to look at the preferences of consumers, the regulated firm looks at the regulatory requirements and tries to capture the regulator (Mueller 2004; Stigler 1971; Peltzman 1976; Etzioni 2009). A financial analyst has aptly pictured this concept: 'When you buy the securities of a utility, you're buying the public utilities commission' (Business Week 1979, p. 114).

From the perspective of organizational science the close relationship (embeddedness) between the regulator and the regulated firms has a strong imprint on the formal and informal organization of regulated firms (Stinchcombe 1965; Johnson 2007). For example, studies of the US electricity industry have shown that tight regulatory oversight leads to a more formal organization of electricity firms, reduced entrepreneurial initiative and paternalistic working relationships (Russo 1992). One might argue that the mindset of the public regulation authority is copied into the organizational routines of the regulated firm. However, imprinting has another effect that is as important as the transfer of organizational routines from the regulator to the regulated firm. Organizational routines are often persistent or path-dependent (Nelson & Winter 1982; Narduzzo & Warglien 2008; Russo 1992). That is, one cannot easily switch from one organizational mode to another or intensify incentives in order to promptly enforce an efficient output of regulated firms. For example, if a public utility has no performance-based career system, such a career system will not emerge overnight. Instead, there will be a period of transition before external incentives become mirrored by organizational routines and external incentives can pass through organizational structures.

In summary, in energy markets it can neither be assumed that organizational structures adapt automatically to the transaction cost minimal solution nor that a regulator can easily implement a smart regulation, which is mimicking market incentives. On the contrary, the market failure of natural monopoly is mirrored persistently in the organizational structure of energy firms. From this follows that the regulation of energy firms involves insightful external incentive regulation as well as the complementary fine-tuning of internal organization, in order to pass external incentives through the organizational structure to the decision-making agent.

5.1.4 *Looking inside the 'black box' – a research agenda*

As it turns out, incentive regulation of energy firms has to take into account organizational issues, in order to be effective and to pass through incentives to the decision-making agent. This problem has been aptly pointed out by Verma, Mitnick and Marcus (1999, p. 408): 'Although the theory [i.e., incentive regulation] predicts effects because of managers' self-interested objectives, the incentive programs built into the newer regulation produce incentives for the firm, not necessarily for individual managers.'

In the following the interplay between external regulation, organization and individual decision making will be elucidated in more detail by highlighting some important problems, which have been until now largely neglected in the literature on incentive regulation. The aim is to set up a research agenda for the analysis of the 'black box' of energy firms. It will become clear that behavioural issues on the organizational and individual level are important factors which have to be considered if one is out to make incentive regulation a successful tool for energy market regulation.

Clarity and comprehensibility of incentives. Incentive schemes work more properly if the targeted results are well defined and the causal link between incentives and the subsequent (re)actions of energy firms are verifiable (Kahneman, Slovic & Tversky 1982; London 2003; Léon 1997). This seemingly facile finding of social psychology has important consequences for the applied control mechanisms of regulation. That is, even if the relation between the regulator and the regulatee is complex and outcomes are opaque, all kinds of behaviour control, like the obligation not to discriminate competitors when grid capacities are allocated, should be complemented by outcome control (Verma,

Mitnick & Marcus 1999; Eisenhardt 1985). A robust outcome measure is, for example, the indication of how many grid capacities were allocated to competitors. Outcome control is preferable, because clear-cut defined regulatory outcomes (e.g., '40 percent of the grid capacity shall be allocated to competitors') help to prevent a subtle deviation from the initially defined regulatory aims. Such deviations are likely because the sometimes strong ties between the regulator and the regulated firms may allow energy firms to influence the regulator and to obtain relaxations of initial regulations. For example, former managers of energy firms frequently become members of the regulation authority. This allows former managers to thwart regulation and to conserve the monopoly profits of energy firms (Knittel 2006). This 'regulatory capture' (Stigler 1971) may be prevented if the aims of regulation are made transparent and verifiable by the public.

Another point is that incentives should be straightforward and comprehensible (Pfeifenberger & Tye 1995). This requirement, again, is in line with findings in research on organizational behaviour and social psychology (Kahneman, Slovic & Tversky 1982; Léon 1997). Straightforwardness and comprehensibility are important ingredients of incentive schemes because the recipients of incentives will more easily adapt to those incentives. That is, only if the regulatee understands the working of the incentive scheme, he will be able to respond properly and fulfil the aims of regulation. In addition, a plain and clear-cut incentive scheme is also advantageous for the regulator because it is easier to control energy firms if the yardstick of regulation is not ambiguous and subject to different interpretations.

Clarity and comprehensibility of incentive schemes seem to be evident or even trivial requirements of incentive regulation. However, in reality, these requirements are frequently ignored (Pfeifenberger & Tye 1995; Buechner & Katzfey 2006). For example, the British regulation of electricity grid firms employs an incentive formula that aims at considering numerous characteristics of grid firms in order to determine the optimal incentive. The formula is supposed to establish optimal incentives for grid firms, leading to an increase in productivity. In addition, the formula aims to cover the costs of running the grid and ensuring a secure supply of energy (for the complete formula, see OFGEM 2008).

Every term in the formula for the British 'revenue cap' has its justification and has been discussed at length in academic and political circles, as well as by the scientific board of the OFGEM (Office of Gas and Electricity Markets). However, one can ask whether the complexity of the formula and the manifold data needed to feed the formula may thwart the aim of setting optimal incentives and achieving efficient regulatory outcomes. What is still missing in the debate on incentive regulation is a more detailed discussion of other straightforward instruments of incentive regulation. Those other instruments of incentive regulation may not be as sophisticated as the current incentive schemes, yet these other incentive schemes might be highly effective (for an early statement see Pfeifenberger & Tye 1995).

Incentive compatibility. Another important point on the research agenda is the compatibility between the 'external' incentives of energy regulation and the aims of decision makers 'within' the firm.

Incentive compatibility requires that decision makers can satisfy their individual preferences and reach their goals within the constraints of organizational structures. If external regulation does not respect individual preferences, then regulation may produce unintended consequences (Verma, Mitnick & Marcus 1999). For example, under a 'legal unbundling' regime, the career of a grid manager may depend on the manager's contribution to the overall profit of the holding company. However, if there is the legal obligation to give non-discriminatory access to the grid for competitors of the holding company, then the manager of the grid firm faces a severe trade-off. On the one hand, the manager may comply with regulation, taking into account the possibility that his career may deteriorate. On the other hand, the manager can apply sophisticated tools of discrimination in order to derogate the competitors of the holding company, which may increase his career chances but may also expose him to the risk of being punished by the regulator. To be clear, whether grid managers decide on one or the other option depends on a multitude of factors, but the trade-off points again to the crucial interdependence of organization and external regulation.

In order to attain incentive compatibility between 'external' regulations and the goals of managers one has to adequately design the organization of grid firms. An economic toolbox for organizational design is provided by 'mechanism design' (Groves & Ledyard 1987), which in recent years has got a lot of attention for a proper regulation of energy markets (Silva, Wollenberg & Zheng 2001; Battle & Perez-Arriaga 2008). The idea is to 'manipulate' the environment of managers in a way that they behave in a manner that is compatible with the aims of regulation. However, mechanism design relies strongly on the assumption of rationality and selfishness of agents (Groves & Ledyard 1987), which may be seen as an obstacle to applying this concept to real world problems (McFadden 2009), when agents are embedded in complex organizational structures. Therefore it is useful to analyse the problem of incentive compatibility also from the perspective of organizational science. From that perspective an agent will align the goals of regulation with his own goals, if sense-making is possible (Weick, Sutcliffe & Obstfeld 2005). Sense-making is possible, if the agent can attribute to regulations, organizational structures or other institutions a sort of inherent logic and legitimacy. If institutional settings make sense, then the agent is more willing to accept regulations and to adapt his behaviour to the logic of institutional constraints. For example, incentive regulation may be obeyed more easily if the regulation scheme makes sense not only from the perspective of cutting the costs of the power grid, but also if incentive regulation is in accordance with environmental protection and if cutting costs does not threat the jobs in the energy sector.

Magnitude and reliability of incentives. Managers of grid firms will be more likely to comply with regulations if the magnitude of regulations is strong and if the regulations are reliable. This proposition is intuitive and has been recently proved by experimental studies of mechanism design (McFadden 2009).

Organizational design has a significant effect on the magnitude of regulatory incentives. For example, under a regime of 'legal unbundling' the regulator may decide that the profits of the grid firm have to be reinvested into the power grid and should be not transferred to the parent company. Such a legal obligation diminishes the incentive to disinvest into the grid and to lower the net capacity, while it strengthens the incentive to allocate the capacity of the power grid efficiently. Under a regime of 'ownership unbundling' the incentive for the managers of the grid firm to disinvest into the power grid can be even higher, in order to obtain – at least for a short term – a high rate of return. Therefore, even stronger legal obligations seem to be in order to counterbalance the incentive to disinvest into the grid capacity. This means that organizational design gives different weights to the various incentives that are in play and the regulator has to target 'organization-sensitive' regulations, in order to achieve the desired regulatory outcome.

Also the reliability of regulations is of great importance to the targeting of incentives (Stern 1997; Hall, Scott & Hood 2000). This point entails several aspects. The first is that incentives have to be enduring and must be repeated so that decision makers can adapt their behaviour. The second is that incentives must not be subject to renegotiations. That is, managers should make an effort to adapt their behaviour and not attempt to manipulate regulations. The third aspect is that rewards from regulatory compliance must follow promptly, in order to underscore the causal link between regulatory compliance and rewards.

The magnitude and reliability of incentives mirror a well-known pair of parameters in economics that has especially been applied in the economic theory of crime (Becker 1968). The first is the level of punishment, and the second is the likelihood of detection. While the magnitude of the incentives may be interpreted as the level of punishment, the reliability of the incentives can be interpreted as the likelihood of one's becoming detected in committing a crime. The stronger the magnitude of the incentives and the higher the reliability of the regulation, the more compliance with regulation can be expected. Even if one is of the opinion that organizational behaviour is not the result of such a simple calculus, the magnitude and reliability of incentives are important parameters for the organizational design of grid firms.

However, one can ask whether organizational science can add further insights to the interplay of organizational structure and the magnitude and reliability of regulation. An important argument is coined by DiMaggio and Powell (1983, p. 152). They hold that organizations 'tend to model themselves after similar organizations in their field that they perceive to be more legitimate or successful.' That is, grid firms may adapt their organizational structure in response to the magnitude and reliability of regulation; however, the attained organizational form may be not the result of a firm's considerations how to improve its efficiency. The organizational form may be more influenced by 'mimetic' processes that focus on well established and widely accepted organizational routines and structures. If that argument by DiMaggio and Powell were true, then aspects of embeddedness and acceptance of organizational routines must be taken into consideration, when one is out to determine the efficient mix of the magnitude and reliability of incentives. For example, under a regime of legal unbundling, bonus wages which are linked to the overall profit of the parent company may lead to inefficient behaviour of grid managers. Managers may be tempted to discriminate competitors of the parent company, in order to maximize the overall profit of the parent company. Therefore those bonus wage systems are forbidden in most countries. However, this sort of bonus wage system may be seen by managers as the appropriate one for controlling affiliated companies, and denying it to managers of grid firms may be considered by them as unfair. As a consequence the prohibition of this bonus wage system can provoke sophisticated counter actions of energy firms, in order to circumvent the prohibition of certain bonus wage systems.

Authorization. Managers have to be authorized to take all appropriate measures in order to react to incentive regulation in a co-ordinated manner. For example, under an incentive regulation regime, grid managers have to decide on two important things: (1) the access price for using the grid and (2) the budgeting of investments in the grid. It is obvious that these two tasks are highly interrelated. The access price, in combination with the grid capacity, determines the potential profit of the grid firm. On the other hand, the grid capacity depends on the investments in the grid. Therefore, the management of access prices and investments in the grid should be bundled as part of the same division, in order for there to be integrated management of grid capacities and access prices.

If the authority to react to incentive regulation is organizationally split (for example, if the planning of investments in the grid occurs in the finance division while the determination of access prices occurs in the sales division), then there may occur severe friction that complicates proper reaction to incentive regulation. The external incentive will be diffused in the organizational structure of grid firms, and incentive regulation may provoke contradictory reactions. The finance division may plan for an extension of the net capacity, while the sales division may plan with a constant net capacity. Although it is somewhat overstated, this simple example makes clear that the allocation of authority plays a crucial role not only in the proper processing of incentive regulation in organizational structures but also in deriving a consistent strategy for how to react on incentive regulation.

Legitimacy. Legitimacy plays an important role in the implementation of incentive schemes. By the term 'legitimacy' in general is meant a procedural quality of organization that relates to democratic accountability (participation), the separation of powers, transparency, and the rule of law (Coglianese 2007). That is, an organization is seen as legitimate if it is in accordance with the basic principles of the social organization of men, if it is embedded in the larger institutional context of societal living (Aguilera & Jackson 2003; Granovetter 1985) and if there are no contradictions between societal and organizational rules. Thereby, legitimacy does not have to be in conflict with economic efficiency. However, there can be conflicts if organizational rules enforce efficient behaviour but this sort of behaviour is not in accordance with the moral frame or accepted routines of society. In such a case, efficient behaviour is seen as illegitimate.

The crucial point is that economic consequences of incentive regulations that are regarded as illegitimate may provoke organizational behaviour that runs against the proper working of incentive regulation. An illustration can be found in Germany. In the past, German energy firms granted ample extra benefits to their employees, like high wages, generous pension plans, broad social security programs, child care for children of employees, et cetera. In addition, energy firms supported communal events like music festivals or sporting events. With the advent of the deregulation of the energy sector and the beginning of incentive regulation, all these extra costs have come under scrutiny because such costs are not directly related to the production, distribution and sale of energy. However, cutting these extra costs is regarded as illegitimate by workers and other beneficiaries, like local communities, because these extra benefits are seen as social achievements that are important components of worker-oriented and democratic firms (Mitbestimmung 2006). Therefore, labour unions and shareholding communities exert pressure on executive managers via the board to preserve these extra-social benefits by emphasizing the corporate social responsibility of energy firms.

Also in New Zealand legitimacy played a role, when (local) grid firms, which are owned by consumer trusts, were exempted from incentive regulation.[11] The explanation was that in case of trust ownership all benefits would automatically accrue to consumers. In addition, consumers will feel responsible for a proper working of management and be motivated to watch a management's price settings. That is, consumers can directly participate in a grid firm's decisions and the management is directly accountable. Hence a redundant control of those grid firms by the regulator is seen not only to be unnecessary, but an additional layer of regulation is considered as illegitimate (Lewis & Meade 2007).

In general, legitimacy points to the important fact that besides efficiency also other normative considerations may play a role, when one is out to regulate an industry. Disregarding legitimacy issues may hamper the proper implementation of incentive regulation severely.

Corporate culture. Corporate culture and work attitudes also play an essential role in the effectiveness of incentive channelling. In the past, energy firms were seen as vertically integrated natural monopolies that were co-ordinated mostly by the commands of civil servants. The influence of civil servants had a strong imprinting effect on the corporate culture of energy firms, which adopted a corporate culture very similar to that of the regulating bureaucracy (Russo 1992).

11 Meanwhile, also consumer owned grid firms are subject to incentive regulation, which caused a public debate on the legitimacy of public regulation.

The interconnection of energy firms with the regulating body put forth a sort of corporate culture less oriented to the needs of consumers, but to the needs of politics. In addition, corporate culture of energy firms does not regard competition as an important part of a market economy but instead is strongly adapted to the accuracy of bureaucratic procedures (DiMaggio & Anheier 1990). Therefore, incentive regulation must cope with a corporate culture that processes incentives like a bureaucratic subunit. In addition, in the past, key positions of energy firms were occupied by engineers who were more interested in a secure supply of energy than in cutting costs. As a consequence, the changes to more market-oriented regulation have often been hampered by engineers in management positions (Mueller & Carter 2007).

The bureaucratic culture of energy firms has been amplified in the past by the application of cost-plus regulation. Cost-plus regulation has led to a situation in which energy firms could not make any profits but also would not see any losses. That is, profit-making did not have the same importance in the energy industry that it did in other industries, or else it was not seen as relevant at all. This situation had a lasting imprinting effect on the corporate culture of energy firms, too (DiMaggio & Anheier 1990). The parent company of a grid firm that is not profitable under incentive regulation may not put it under pressure to become more efficient because the management of the parent company may 'forgive' the management of the grid firm. Managers of parent companies of grid firms are more likely to forgive inefficiencies because they often contain the old routines of cost-plus regulation within themselves (Russo 1992), although cost-plus regulation has come to an end.

In sum, corporate culture and work attitudes constitute a set of important but complex problems that are of the utmost importance when one is aiming to make incentive regulation work. Even if one is of the opinion that, in the end, the corporate culture of energy firms will converge towards that of firms in ordinary markets, the corporate culture of energy firms represents a set of special problems that have to be overcome in the transition period from highly regulated markets to deregulated ones.

5.1.5 *Summing-up*

On a conceptual level the relation between external regulations and organizational structure is not really problematic as long as firms are operating in markets without market failures. Firms that are not able to adapt their organizational structure to the needs of external regulations will face bankruptcy. In competitive markets there is always a pool of experimenting firms trying to find the best organizational structures for the adequate channelling of incentives. Therefore, from a macro perspective, the interplay between external regulation and organizational structure has not received much attention in the past (Kole & Lehn 1997, 1999).

However, the need to understand in which way external regulation and organizational structure interact increases sharply if the automatic processing of external incentives through the organizational structure of firms to the decision-making agent becomes systematically blocked. That happens when there is no pool of firms competing with differentiated products and different organizational structures but when there is a natural monopoly. Now the regulator must consider the connection between external regulation and organizational structure.

A major problem for analyzing the connection between external regulation and organizational structure seems to be the neoclassical framework that is imposed on the analysis of energy markets. It turns out that there are two important restrictions of neoclassical analysis. The first is the 'black box' view of firms. The second is the idea that agents always make rational choices. One may discuss at length whether rational choice models can reflect reality well enough in order to derive meaningful propositions. However, here it is argued that it is useful to complement rational choice analysis with insights of organizational behaviour, in order to achieve a more nuanced picture of the interrelationship between external and internal incentives. To make this point more accessible, a research agenda has been presented for the analysis of incentive channelling in energy markets. The research agenda highlights several aspects of energy market regulation that cannot be processed using neoclassical theory alone. For sure, the presented research agenda is by no means conclusive; there may be other points that are also of interest for a better understanding of incentive channelling, or the points of the research agenda may be further subdivided for more specialized research questions. However, the conceptual framework and the presented research agenda may be understood as a first step toward a better understanding of the crucial relationship between external regulations and organizational structure in the case of public utilities.

5.2 TORT LIABILITY AND ORGANIZATIONAL DESIGN

5.2.1 *Setting up the problem*

The second example points to the relevance of organizational structure for making better informed group decisions. It will be shown that the probability of making harmful decisions as well as selling defective products depends on a firm's organizational structure. This means, by implication, that a firm may be held liable, if it has not installed an organizational structure which can properly evaluate risks. For example, the safety of an air flight does not only depend on the skills of the pilot, but also on the proper organization of an airplane's technical maintenance. Is it possible to identify attributes of an organizational structure for maintaining airplanes, which properly reflect the risk of operating air flights? And if this would be possible, what would follow from this? In case an airline has adopted an adequate organizational structure for maintaining airplanes, would it then economically be justified that in case of an air crash the airline is not liable? Or, when is it possible and justified to prescribe firms ex ante a certain organizational structure, in order to prevent harm to third parties? Answers to these questions have practical consequences for the efficient design of a firm's organizational architecture as well as for courts, which have to assess a firm's liability. These are very topical questions, which have been raised for example in the event of the loss of the NASA-shuttle 'Columbia' in 2003 (CAIB 2003). Or, it has been questioned whether the organizational structure of the Catholic Church might be responsible for sustaining and covering up the sexual misconduct of priests (France 2004. Or, a nurse mistakes a used syringe for a clean one. In that case it is possible that the wrongdoing is not caused by the negligent nurse but by the organization that has not installed proper safety procedures (Van Boom 2009; Cebul, Rebitzer, Taylor & Votruba 2008).

Besides the challenging theoretical questions which arise of the interplay of liability rules and a firm's organizational structure, there is a recent development in tort law, especially in Europe, which pays more and more attention to organizations as the carriers of potential harmful activities (Van Boom 2009; Koch 2007; Krawiec 2005). In a growing number of European drafts and proposals on tort law 'organizational design' has been introduced as a new category, in order to embrace the fact that often harmful damages are not due to wrongdoings of a single individual, but the consequence of organizational failure.[12] Although

12 See, for example, the French 'Projet Catala' (2005)' and the Austrian draft (Koziol 2006).

the diverse drafts and proposals for reforming European tort laws acknowledge organizational design issues as a new category, these drafts and proposals show a lack of understanding in which way organizational design can be conceptualized as a valid category of tort liability. Also in the United States organizational liability has become a pressing topic. In recent years the incumbent doctrine of vicarious strict liability has been largely complemented and replaced by the Organizational Sentencing Guidelines (OSG) and diverse internal compliance-based liability regimes. Those guidelines prescribe particular codes of conduct for an organization, like ethic codes. If an organization has adopted such a code effectively, the organization may not be held strictly liable.

In the following, in a first step it will be clarified in more detail what is meant by organizational design in relation to a firm's liability. Then, in a second step, it will be shown in which way insights from organizational science can be employed, in order to determine organizational designs which aim at the optimal prevention of damages.

5.2.2 *Organizations as tortfeasors*

Can an organization be held liable if misconduct is in essence always a result of individual actions or decisions? If one assumes that misconduct is the result of an individual's wrongdoing, then organizational liability must be a construct of principal agent relations, where a misconducting agent (individual) is improperly controlled by a principal (organization). The doctrine of vicarious liability exactly applies this contractual framework to define when an organization has to be held liable (Sykes 1984; for an overview see Kraakman 2009).

While ordinarily the negligence of one person cannot be imputed to another person, in an organizational context it can, if there is a particular legal relationship to the person who did act negligently. Those relationships are typically the relationship between parent and child, husband and wife, owner of a vehicle and driver, and employer and employee (West's Encyclopedia of American Law 2008).

Most important in the context of organizations is the doctrine of *respondeat superior*, which is based on the employer-employee relationship and which makes the employer responsible for a lack of care on the part of an employee in relation to those to whom the employer owes a duty of care. The employer is legally responsible for the negligence of the employee, because the employee is an agent of the employer. So, if misconduct is committed by an employee acting within the general scope of the employment, the employer is liable for damages (for a discussion see Sykes 1984). For example, if the driver of a milk delivery truck is involved in an accident, causing injury, the dairy factory will be responsible for the damages if the driver is found to be negligent. Since the company will automatically be found liable if the driver is negligent, the doctrine of *respondeat superior* is a form of strict liability.

In general, vicarious liability makes organizations liable if employees are authorized to make representations of a particular class on behalf of the organization, and if that representation causes a loss to a third party. The organization will be liable even though the particular representation was an improper way of doing what the employer was authorized to do (West's Encyclopedia of American Law 2008).

The basic economic idea of vicarious liability is that by forcing organizations to internalize all costs of their activities, the organization's products are appropriately priced and the socially optimal amount of the good or service is attained (Sykes 1984; for an extension to corporate crime see Fischel & Sykes 1996). From this follows the adoption of the optimal level of internal organizational enforcement and deterrence mechanisms. Since an organization bears all costs of any damages, it has an incentive to reduce the incidence of those damages up to the point where the costs of such reduction equal the benefits (Krawiec 2005; Arlen & Kraakman 1997).

Apparently the principal agent framework of vicarious liability fits nicely into the new institutional economics of the firm. New institutional economics can help to answer the question how to set optimal incentives for an organization's principals to install an efficient monitoring of agents. Or, one can determine which kinds of employment contracts should be enabled and which not in order to make a principal's monitoring of agents most effective. Or, one can determine in which way residual rights of control (property rights) should be designed in order to avoid an inefficient allocation of risk within an organization. For example, the doctrine of *enterprise liability* holds that it is not allowed to shift all risks and damages to one legal entity of the organization, while the returns and benefits of the business are protected in another legal entity. In the event of damages the whole organization (the parent company and all affiliations) will be held liable, in order to prevent organizations from making hazardous risk shifts.

Here it is not possible to go into all details of vicarious liability. However, one important criticism is that vicarious liability may prevent the establishment of proper internal compliance structures, because those structures make it more likely that misconduct becomes detected (Cooter & Ulen 2008, p. 382). This outcome of a liability regime is certainly not socially beneficial. Related to this problem is that often internal compliance structures are seen as not credible by employees, because detecting misconduct is not in the firm's interest, given that an organization is always liable for the misconduct of its employees (Krawiec 2005). In summary, it is questionable whether vicarious liability can optimally deter misconduct of an organization's agents (for a nuanced discussion see Arlen & Kraakman 1997).

In recent years, the critique on vicarious liability has led to a more friendly view on negligence-based organizational liability regimes. Although negligence regimes tend not to internalize the full amount of external costs, because the activity level cannot be controlled (leading to an overproduction of the harmful activity or good), they can in theory induce the optimal level of internal deterrence measures (Krawiec 2005). The reason is that in case a particular compliance measure has been installed, the organization will not be held liable for the wrongdoing of one of its agents. Different from strict vicarious liability an organization has a clear incentive to install compliance measures. Given this advantage of a negligence-based regime, in recent years in the United States the Organizational Sentencing Guidelines (OSG) and other internal compliance-based liability regimes have got a prominent role in the prevention of organizational misconduct.

While vicarious liability leaves it open to organizations to undertake appropriate measures against misconduct of agents, under negligence-based liability a certain standard of care has to be prescribed. This is due to the fact that in case of a wrongdoing a court has to decide whether an organization has applied an optimal standard of care. But because the optimal standard of care is seldom known by courts, it is common to adopt standards which have been drafted by external experts in a field. However, two severe problems arise. (1) Does an outside expert really know better than courts or any other entity, what the optimal standard of care is, say for example, the optimal ethic rules for a car manufacturer? And in addition, if an optimal standard for one firm has been found, will it be equally applicable to all firms of an industry? (2) Organizations may adopt a code of conduct only cosmetically. That is, a court must always verify whether a code of conduct is reliable or only a fake (Krawiec 2003). The mere existence of codes may say nothing about the appropriateness of their content or about their enforcement.

In the end, the literature on organizational liability is not clear on whether a strict vicarious liability regime or a negligence-based regime is more advantageous. Also mixed systems have been proposed, in order to overcome the weaknesses of each liability regime. However, in recent years it has turned out that compliance-based liability regimes have become more and more adopted, while strict vicarious liability regimes have lost terrain (Krawiec 2005).

5.2.3 *Organizational liability from the perspective of organizational science*

From an organizational science perspective vicarious liability as well as internal compliance-based liability regimes are one-dimensional approaches. They transform organizational failure into a more or less complex principal-agent relation between a wrongdoing employee and a monitoring employer. Thereby agents and principals behave as rational profit maximizers. Because in reality firms do maximize profits and individuals do maximize their utility by maximizing their wealth, the incumbent approaches to organizational liability are important safeguards against fraudulent wrongdoings of employees as well as means to set incentives for employers to monitor employees. However, the 'failure rate' of organizational behaviour does not only depend on rationally planned misconduct of individuals. Two lines of argument have been largely neglected so far: (1) Behavioural triggers of misconduct, and (2) co-ordination failures.

The term 'behavioural triggers' refers to the puzzle that it is not easy to explain in terms of principal agent theory, why employees often commit wrongdoings from which the organization benefits, but not the wrongdoer. For example, rogue trading pays especially for the investment company, which receives fees for every transaction. Or, a bribing manager of a building company helps his or her firm to get a job. His or her private benefit is often small compared to the benefit of the firm (Krawiec 2005).

Why should a rational individual behave in such a way? Even though it is argued that the wrongdoer expects a promotion of his or her career in exchange for his or her wrongdoing, it is often doubtful that the committed risks outweigh the expected benefits. This raises the question why some people take risks for the sake of an organization. Which are the behavioural triggers of such behaviour?

On the *individual* level one can explain this sort of irrational behaviour with the help of psychological theories. However, it is also possible to explain 'irrational misconduct' on the *group* level with the help of theories of organizational behaviour. In addition, both levels of analysis can be intertwined and may affect each other.

On the individual level an important trigger for irrational misconduct is a false risk perception of wrongdoers (for an overview, see Slovic

2000). Even if there exist codes of conduct in order to facilitate a correct risk assessment, individuals may tolerate too high risk levels. An individual may systematically underestimate the risk of a transaction, thereby raising the failure rate of the transaction beyond its optimal level. Or, individuals may falsely rely on the expertise of others, who claim that a transaction is within the bandwidth of tolerable risk. The recent financial crisis provides abundant examples of those types of false risk perception, which have caused damages to third parties, but which were not intended to directly enrich the wrongdoer.

But a false risk perception alone cannot explain why some individuals persistently ignore codes of conduct or try to escape the monitoring of their superiors. It is reasonable to assume that over time individuals become more aware of the true risks and will adapt their behaviour as well as employ institutional safeguards, in order to facilitate appropriate behaviour. Codes of conduct and best practices can be understood as those emergent institutions which respond to individual deception.[13] Nevertheless, some individuals do not stop misconduct, even if they are aware that they are acting irrationally. For example, why did Nick Leeson not stop his hazardous financial trades, which led to the collapse of Barings Bank in 1995? This can be explained if one takes into account the psychological dynamics of risk taking. 'Escalating commitment' is a well documented behavioural pattern (Staw 1976; Brockner 1992) where individuals justify increased investment in a decision, based on the cumulative prior investment, despite new evidence suggesting that the costs of continuing the decision outweighs the expected benefit. Nick Leeson tried to cover the losses of his past investments by accepting higher and higher risk levels of his new investments till his 'system' blew up.

Theories of individual behaviour can explain why individuals may commit irrational misconduct. They cannot convincingly explain why organizations have persistent problems to prevent misconduct. For a convincing explanation one needs theories which refer to organizational behaviour. Therefore, in the following, insights from organizational science will be added to the puzzle of organizational liability.

In general, an inefficiently high rate of misconduct can be explained if management positions are filled with individuals who have a high propensity for risk taking, and/or if an organization tolerates overly risky behaviour. Both factors have to do with organizational cul-

13 For a general discussion of the spontaneous emergence of institutions, see Smith (2003).

ture and the environment in which an organization is embedded.

The impact of organizational culture and the environment on misconduct may be best explained by the example of rogue trading. Despite persistent losses for investment firms and third parties and despite diverse codes of conduct and compliance programs, rogue trading is still a prevalent misconduct in the investment trade business (Krawiec 2009). Therefore, one can conjecture that the incumbent liability rules which only aim at individual behaviour are not well equipped to tackle this kind of misbehaviour.

To start with, traders are more devoted to materialism than other professions. This is by nature and nurture (Haucap & Just 2010; Frey, Pommerehne & Gygi 1993). Individuals with a high propensity to materialism are more likely to become traders. But also the climate at the trading floor fosters a materialistic attitude. Successful traders are not rewarded with titles and steps up on the career ladder. The hierarchy of traders is mirrored by how much money a trader can make for the firm and how high the bonuses are compared to others (Krawiec 2000; 2005). Thereby '[m]oney is more than just the medium of exchange; it is a measure of one's "winnings". It provides an identity that prevails over charisma, physical attractiveness, or sociability as the arbiter of success and power on the bond trading floor. The top earning trader is king of the mountain' (Abolafia 1996, p. 30). This attitude leads to both profitable trading for the firm on the one hand and rogue trading on the other.

Besides the individual attributes of traders the industry's level of competiveness plays a crucial role in amplifying rogue trading. The trading business attracts and selects individuals who have the attributes of competitive traders, but who also have a propensity for rogue trading. March and Shapira (1987, p. 1414) have pointed to this fact: 'Although [managers] undoubtedly vary in their individual propensities to take risks, those variations are obscured by processes of selection that reduce the heterogeneity among managers and encourage them to believe in their ability to control the odds, by systems of organizational controls and incentives that dictate risk taking behavior in significant ways, and by variations in the demand for risk taking produced by the context within which choice takes place.' In the end the trading business is occupied with individuals taking high risk levels, who tend to systematically disregard codes of conduct.

Finally, one can ask if not superiors may be the ones who have to guarantee that traders refrain from wrongdoings. However, it cannot be expected that superiors put much effort in monitoring traders. An important reason is that superiors have the same imprint as traders. Most of them are senior traders or have been attached to the trading business for years. In other words, their morale and attitude is not very different from the one of floor traders. Superiors may be not of the opinion that their primary obligation is the supervision of traders, but to maximize the account of the company and to get bonuses as much as possible (Krawiec 2005). For example, in 2003 employees of Prudential Financial, Inc. were charged with securities fraud in connection with mutual fund market-timing trades. The traders claimed in court that the management as well as the compliance department knew of the trades and rewarded them for the fees they brought in (Krawiec 2005; Barboza 2003). Another example is Salomon Brothers Inc., which after its rogue-trading scandal in 1994 revised its incentive pay system severely. The liquidity of bonuses was considerably reduced. As a consequence, after the announcement twenty of its two hundred managing directors quitted their jobs taking with them a number of top traders. Finally, Salomon Brothers stopped its plan to implement a new reward system (Krawiec 2005). That is, traders are not only looking for a place where they can make a lot of money, but where it is also possible to act out their competitive attitude.[14]

In summary, organizational culture turns out as a decisive factor for risk taking and to commit misconduct (Sitkin & Pablo 1992). Since organizational culture is an informal institution, it cannot be easily changed by the will of a rule maker or by drafting mission statements (Zenger, Lazzarini & Poppo 2002; Lazzarini, Miller & Zenger, 2004). In addition, shared norms and believes can undermine formal rules, making them largely ineffective. As a consequence, any formal ruling concerned with organizational liability is well advised to take into account organizational behaviour, in order to facilitate the implementation and workability of formal liability rules.

Besides 'behavioural triggers of misconduct', 'co-ordination failures' can lead to organizational misconduct. In case of co-ordination failures, individual misconduct traces back to an inferior co-ordination of organizational activities. Thereby the efficacy of co-ordinating activities largely depends on organizational design, which decides on the degree of centralization or decentralization of activities as well as the degree of autonomy an organizational layer has.

14 For a discussion of the psychological triggers leading to competitive behaviour of traders see McClelland (1961, 1987).

Starting with daily experience one may guess that organizational design surely has an impact on a firm's level of precautions against harmful wrongdoing. The ad hoc rationale for this appraisal may be that daily routine teaches us that organizational structure matters. Whenever you are in contact with an organization, like a computer manufacturer, a warehouse, a hospital or a university, you get the impression that the performance of the specific organization is highly influenced by the organization's architecture. For example, you may have had the experience that a more decentralized organizational structure may lead to more flexible responses of that organization, while the quality of the organization's services often seems to be low or arbitrary. On the other hand, a more hierarchical organization may be much slower and inflexible in processing a customer's request, but in most cases the quality of services is fine and more standardized. One reason could be that in a more decentralized organization employees have more autonomy and are entitled to decide on a broader range of issues, while in a hierarchical organization decision making on a certain level of organization is constrained by the oversight of superior organizational levels. And you may conclude that these experiences may also apply to a firm's dealings with tort liability. You may wonder whether a decentralized or a hierarchical organizational design may be better, in order to attain an efficient level of precautionary measures. However, drawing conclusions from daily life experience is ad hoc and can be misleading. Therefore, a better theoretical understanding of the interplay between liability rules and organizational design is needed.

A first idea could be that co-ordination failures may exist. However, market forces will put organizations under pressure to adopt those organizational structures which lead to an optimal failure rate of organizations. Especially in case of vicarious liability, a firm has to take into account all costs of economic activity and therefore it has a strong incentive to manage for an organizational design which calibrates the costs of being held liable on an optimal level. For example, if it pays to have an additional organizational layer for the detection of product failures, then a firm will adapt its organizational design. Otherwise, firms that cannot manage for a sufficient degree of organizational efficiency will face bankruptcy (Alchian 1950; Friedman 1953; Vromen 1995). However, there are two important restrictions of this argument. Firstly, market selection is workable in the long run, but may not trigger efficiency in the short run. Secondly, there may be market failures which prevent a proper processing of incentives through the organizational structure to the decision-making agent (cf. section 4.1).

Even if one agrees to the general idea that market forces will press firms to adapt their organizational design towards efficiency, this argument is only valid in its strong form, if a market structure of perfect competition exists (Boland 2003; Singh 2003). Only then, market forces will ensure an immediate adaptation of the organizational design towards efficiency. In case the model of perfect competition does not apply, it is a matter of degree whether there is an adaptation of organizational design towards efficiency and how long this process takes. Since market failures are ubiquitous and the prerequisites of perfect competition are never fulfilled in reality, it turns out that firms can choose from a range of organizational designs without being instantly punished by market forces. This means that it is possible that at the same time there are different organizational designs in place which have the same efficacy.

But co-ordination failures do not only depend on the workability of competition in an industry. One can also ask whether a liability rule may more directly trigger organizational disruptions, which lead to a higher rate of misconduct.

It has been argued that vicarious liability will set optimal incentives for an organization to undertake appropriate measures against misconduct (Sykes 1984; Arlen & Kraakman 1997). However, vicarious liability may produce efficiency reducing incentives to an organization itself. Thereby, it is not blatant misconduct of single individuals which causes organizational failure, but the failure to co-ordinate organizational activities in a proper way. This can be best illustrated with the help of an example.

A hospital's performance in terms of effective treatments, a high rate of curing diseases as well as running the hospital costs effectively depends to a high degree on the vertical and horizontal organization of medical services. For example, the cardiac department must closely co-ordinate with the radiation department, the surgery department, the physiotherapy department and a lot of other services. It is obvious that an effective co-ordination will inevitably need some sort of vertical oversight, in order to align the different departmental services. That is, a body with central power is necessary for lifting a hospital's full capacity of medical treatment.

In the United States vicarious liability undermines a proper organization of medical services of hospitals. The reason is that in case of medical malpractice the hospital is liable if it is the employer of physicians. This means that in case the hospital has the right to co-ordinate the services of physicians then it will be strictly liable for the negligence of one of its physicians. As a consequence hospitals are reluctant to employ physicians, in order to prevent being held liable for malpractice (Cebul, Rebitzer, Taylor & Votruba 2008). The drawback of this practice is the impairment of organizational co-ordination and ultimately a higher probability of malpractice. This becomes pretty clear in the following statement: 'The ancillary services that contribute to medical treatment of the patient are usually performed by hospital employees. If a hospital may not legally practice medicine, may it practice nursing or pharmacy? How is the hospital to direct and correlate and make them available to the physician when he needs them in the treatment of his patient? It is essential if hospitals are to continue as centers of organized medical care, that their governing boards have authority to exercise the kinds of control over personnel – including certain professional personnel – without which the boards cannot discharge their responsibility to make the various services available when they are needed.' (Willcox 1960, pp. 433; see also Kusserow 1991).

In the past a multitude of contractual models have been employed with which physicians became enabled to work in a hospital. However, all these models (for an overview see Jacobi & Huberfeld 2001; Janulis & Hornstein 1985) foreclose a direct contractual relation between the physician and the hospital. The result is widespread organizational inefficiency from which patients suffer as well as society, which is the ultimate cost bearer of an inefficient organization of health care.

Surely, in recent years the increasing need of more vertical direction led to new organizational forms, in order to better integrate physicians into a hospital's operations. However, also these new organizational modes largely fail to set incentives for physicians to invest in relationship specific human capital investments and to co-ordinate their services within a hospital (Cebul, Rebitzer, Taylor & Votruba 2008). 'The structures that were put in place to integrate hospitals, primary care providers, and specialists often failed to fundamentally alter the manner in which physicians practiced medicine and collaborated with other health care professionals (that is, "clinical integration"). As a result, integrated structures rarely integrated the actual delivery of patient care.' (Burns & Pauly 2002, p. 134). In summary, strict vicarious liability turns out as a legal hindrance to a proper organization of hospital services.

One may discuss in theory at length whether strict vicarious liability sets the optimal incentives for potential wrongdoers and their superiors to avoid misconduct, if a particular organizational design is exogenously given. However, in reality organizational design is not exogenously given, but endogenously co-determined by liability rules.

From this follows that the choice and design of liability rules have an impact on the efficacy of an organization's processes. Maladapted organizational processes raise the failure rate of organizations, because individual behaviour is largely determined by the organizational design which specifies what an organizational member is allowed to do and what not.

One may ask whether negligence-based liability rules lead to a better co-ordination of an organization's activities. Negligence-based liability may prevent the strategic contracting out of services and processes which should be vertically integrated within one firm. But so far the prescription of codes of conduct is almost exclusively aimed at the behaviour of single individuals. Organizational design issues play only a minor role, and when they do, those design issues are mainly concerned with safeguarding the implementation of a code (e.g. ombudsman, compliance officer). Or, it is vaguely stated that organizations should adapt an efficient design. For example, the Dutch Law on Quality in Health Care Organizations (endorsed in 1996) formulates the requirement that the structure of health care organizations should be such that it allows the delivery of responsible care (Van Gennip & Sillevis Smitt 2000). But it is left open which organizational design will support responsible care or at which organizational design a health care organization should aim in general. In addition, it is difficult to imagine under negligence-based liability that a jurisdiction can ex ante prescribe an organizational design for every firm within an industry which minimizes organizational failure. This would be apparently the 'pretence of knowledge' (Hayek 1989) and one wonders how such a system could be administered by state agencies and courts.

In summary, today neither strict vicarious liability nor negligence-based liability can cope with misconduct which is the result of organizational failure. On the contrary, liability rules can be the source of organizational failure.

5.2.4 *Structural remedies against organizational misconduct*

If one accepts that a maladapted organizational design can be a separate source of wrongdoing, then the question arises what this means for the design of tort law and what organizational science can contribute to tort law.

First of all, the task is not to replace strict vicarious liability or negligence-based liability. It is hard to see how these principles could be replaced by a different system. Both approaches have their pros and cons and can under certain circumstances set proper incentives for individuals to avoid misconduct and to calibrate damages on an optimal level. Therefore, organizational design is a category which is not a substitute but a complementary device, in order to improve organizational liability. However, this alone has far reaching consequences.

While vicarious liability does not care about organizational design, the introduction of organizational design as a distinct category leads to the idea that a court has to evaluate whether a firm has adopted an appropriate organizational design, in order to avoid misconduct. This implies in some form or another that there will be elements of negligence-based liability, even though vicarious liability may apply in general. For example, there may be rewards for firms which can demonstrate that they have applied an appropriate organizational design, in order to avoid misconduct. Those composite regimes have already been proposed to align vicarious liability and negligence-based regimes (Krawiec 2005; Arlen & Kraakman 1997). In addition, those rewards might be an incentive for firms to search for organizational designs, which bring down organizational misconduct to an optimal level.

Even if it is possible to identify organizational design as a separate category in tort law, the question remains which kind of organizational design might be the appropriate one in a specific case. Given that industries and single firms differ largely, it seems impossible to prescribe any organizational design. In addition, firms do not only compete by their products and services but also by their different organizational designs, which multiplies organizational diversity.

Nevertheless, it might be possible to identify industry specific organizational design standards which broadly indicate that a certain kind of organizational design might be preferable in order to reduce the failure of organizational misconduct. To answer this question, one has to ask organizational science and try to find out whether it is possible to derive some general insights on organizational design and the prevention of harm.

While all human beings can make wrong decisions and may cause harmful injuries to others, organizational design can be a powerful means of checks and balances to prevent individual wrongdoing and to promote decisions which are efficiency enhancing. For example, a firm's R&D department has developed a new pharmaceutical, which promises a new treatment against cancer. The head of the R&D department is enthusiastic and reports to the chief executive officer all the positive characteristics of the new pharmaceutical, thereby underestimating the fact that the new drug may cause severe adverse reactions. If the head of the R&D department has a strong position in the firm's hierarchy or if the chief executive officer believes strongly in the reports of the R&D department, then the likelihood increases that a potentially defective product will be sold, and in the end the firm may be liable for paying enormous amounts of compensation. On the other hand, if the chief executive officer impedes the marketing of the new pharmaceutical because of the threat of being held liable for selling a defective product, although a more exact investigation would have shown that the adverse effects are rather small, then the firm not only forfeits a profit, but cancer sufferers may miss the chance of being cured. In both cases organizational design is responsible for a welfare reducing outcome: In the first case the new pharmaceutical is introduced, even though its social costs overbalance its social benefits, and in the second case the drug is not marketed, although the social benefits exceed the social costs.

This simple example points to the crucial role of information and allocating authority within an organizational architecture. In essence optimal decisions depend on the information an organizational architecture is able to generate and to process, in order to cope with individual human fallibility.

An organizational theory which explicitly deals with human fallibility and the question in which way organizational design can cope with the fact of human bounded rationality is that of hierarchies and polyarchies (Sah & Stiglitz 1985; 1986; Sah 1991; Koh 1992; Christensen & Knudsen 2010). This organizational theory deals with the question whether it is possible to minimize false human decisions by the help of organizational architectures which filter information and allocate decision-making authority.

Surely, in order to understand the working of organizations one can draw on a multiplicity of organizational theories. Roughly one can distinguish between neoclassical and behavioural approaches, and one can fiercely debate which of these approaches has more explanatory power. In this regard the advantage of the theory of organizational architecture is that it makes no specific assumptions about human nature; the only assumption is that humans can make wrong decisions. Wrong decisions may owe to limited information, cognitive limitations or biased processing of information. However, organizational architecture is a means to cope with that problem.

In theory it is possible to design organizations with a perfect hierarchy and a perfect filtering of information (Sah & Stiglitz 1985; 1986). The idea is that in a hierarchical organization it is less likely that a harmful activity will be performed, because of the hierarchical filters an activity has to pass. Only when a proposed activity has positively passed the evaluation of different organizational layers, this activity will be performed. But a hierarchical organization is also reluctant against innoxious activities, which also causes a welfare loss. On the other hand, a decentralized organization is more likely to allow wrongful activities, but also innoxious activities have a better chance to pass. That is, hierarchies and polyarchies are committed to different kinds of failures. This allows for a purposeful filtering of information by combining hierarchical and decentralized organizational layers in a resourceful way.

However, in reality a perfect organizational design and filtering of information is not meaningful, because a multiplicity of organizational layers will slow down the decision-making process and will lead to high transaction costs. Therefore, it is necessary to determine case specific organizational designs that equilibrate the costs and benefits of performing a harmful activity on a socially optimal level. Those specific organizational designs can then be used as a benchmark, in order to decide whether the actual organizational design of a specific firm is appropriate to tackle the risk of the performed activities or not.

To be sure, firm heterogeneity and market dynamics prevent any third party from easily determining which organizational design would have been the optimal one, in order to calibrate damages on an optimal level. However, the approach of hierarchies and polyarchies proposed by Sah and Stiglitz is nevertheless promising. It provides a stylized framework, which makes no specific assumptions about human nature. The only assumption is that humans can make wrong decisions, may that be because of rational calculus or because of cognitive limitations.

In a torts case the framework can be used by courts to evaluate whether a firm has employed enough hierarchical checks in order to prevent a wrongdoing. Thereby it is plausible to assume that a risky activity will be associated with a steeper hierarchy than activities with a low risk profile. But the optimal organizational design depends on other variables as well; a decisive role is played by the probability with which agents realize whether or not their decision will cause damage, also the potential profit of a decision affects the organizational design as well as the costs which are associated with filtering information. Taking those variables into account leads to non-trivial propositions about socially optimal organizational designs. Even though a court can only estimate the involved probabilities, profits and costs, the proposed framework can contribute to a substantiated statement whether a firm has adopted an organizational structure which can prudentially cope with potential wrongdoings. In addition, the framework can also be helpful for firms which want to prove that they have undertaken appropriate steps to inhibit organizationally driven misconduct. Another application of the framework may be the development of 'benchmark designs' as a sort of standards for whole industries, which can be used to evaluate whether a firm which belongs to a certain industry has adopted a proper organizational design.

Finally, differently to codes of conduct, which are the backbone of present negligence-based organizational liability, structural standards aiming at the organizational design are more reliable. This means that structural solutions become more visible to third parties and the compliance with those structures can be better verified. For example, hierarchical relations can be identified in employment contracts, organization charts, specific directions of superiors, or contracts of domination between firms. It is hard to imagine a firm which only pretends a formal organizational structure, while it is easy to imagine that codes of conduct are only cosmetic (Krawiec 2005).

5.2.5 *Summing-up*

Organizational design has yet not received very much attention as a distinct category in the law and economics analysis of tort law. This is surely a research gap which is worth to be filled in the future; not in the least because there are several reform projects on tort law on the way, which address organizational design issues without any theoretical underpinning.

Basically, organizational failure results from 'behavioural triggers' and 'co-ordination failures'. Behavioural triggers comprise individual as well as organizational dispositions which lead to misconduct. Especially organizational culture seems to be a decisive factor for the propensity of individuals to commit a wrongdoing. Unfortunately, up to now the meaning of organizational culture for designing liability rules has played no systematic role in the debates about organizational tort liability.

'Co-ordination failures' is another category which up to now has not played any role in organizational tort liability. However, this category is of utmost importance, since liability rules can be the source of severe co-ordination failures, as the example of hospital services in the United States reveals.

It is by no means easy to make recommendations how tort law should be designed and amended, in order to tackle organizational liability. But it seems pretty clear that law and economics could learn from the insights of organizational science. In particular the behavioural theory of the firm has a stock of knowledge that could be of great importance to tort law. Besides behavioural approaches there are also more structural approaches available, which can help to identify those organizational structures that bring down misconduct to an optimal level. However, yet those approaches are not very well developed, but they open a new direction for future research how to think about the problem of organizational liability.

6. A BRIEF OUTLOOK ON TWO MEETING DISCIPLINES

At the beginning of this essay a retrospective was presented on the departing of economics and organizational science. But one may ask whether in the future there will be the chance that both disciplines will be united again. A reunification of the disciplines could yield enormous theoretical and practical benefits. This essay is an attempt to sketch out these benefits.

Yet, it is unclear whether there will be a reunification at all and if so, in which way it could take place. However, there are signals that organizational science issues get more attention in economics in general and in law and economics in particular. For example, recently Posner (2010a) contributed the lead article to a special issue of the Journal of Institutional Economics. The programmatic title of Posner's article is: 'From the new institutional economics to organization economics: with applications to corporate governance, government agencies, and legal institutions'. Although neither Posner nor his discussants made any reference to the behavioural theory of the firm,[15] it becomes pretty clear that organizational issues get increasingly more attention in law and economics. This is underpinned by Posner who writes: 'I have tried to show that organization economics has much to add to our understanding of organizations that are of special interest to law; and, so focused, organizational economics blends into "law and economics" (that is, economic analysis of law). Those organizations are various; [...]. In all these examples, we have seen the organization attempting to align the conduct of the organization's employees with the organization's goals – and in all we have seen the attempt falter because of inherent limitations of the organization as a method of motivating and structuring economic and other activity. Many organizational features of the legal system remain to be studied with the tools of organization economics sketched in this paper.' (Posner 2010a, p. 31)[16] Posner's statement shall mark the end of this essay.

Ik heb gezegd.

---

15 Frey (2010) comes in his comment on Posner very close to the position of the behavioural theory of the firm by pointing to the importance of psychological and sociological issues for a proper understanding of organizations. However, he does not explicitly distinguish between the individual and the group level of decision making, which is centre stage for organizational science.

16 For the importance of organizational issues for law and economics see also Posner (2010b).

LITERATURE

Abolafia, M. (1996): Making markets: opportunism and restraint on Wall Street, Cambridge, Mass.
Acton, J. and Vogelsang, I. (1989): Introduction to "Symposium on Price-Cap Regulation", in: Rand Journal of Economics, Vol. 20, 369-372.
Aguilera, R.V. and Jackson, G. (2003): The Cross-National Diversity of Corporate Governance: Dimensions and Determinants, in: Academy of Management Review, Vol. 28, 447-465.
Alchian, A.A. (1950): Uncertainty, Evolution and Economic Theory, in: Journal of Political Economy, Vol. 58, 211-221.
Alchian, A.A. and Demsetz, H. (1972): Production, Information Costs, and Economic Organization, in: American Economic Review, Vol. 62, 777-795.
Arcuri, A. (2008): Eclecticism in Law and Economics, in: Erasmus Law Review, Vol. 1, 59-81.
Argote, L. and Greve, H.R. (2007): A Behavioral Theory of the Firm – 40 years and counting: Introduction and impact, in: Organization Science, Vol. 18, 337-349.
Arlen, J.H. and Kraakman, R. (1997): Controlling corporate misconduct: An analysis of corporate liability regimes, in: New York University Law Review, Vol. 72, 687-779.
Arrow K.J. and Debreu, G. (1954): The Existence of an Equilibrium for a Competitive Economy, in: Econometrica, Vol. 23, 265-290.
Augier, M. (2004): March'ing towards "a behavioral theory of the firm", in: Management Decision, Vol. 42, 1257-1268.

Batlle, C. and Perez-Arriaga, I.J. (2008): Design criteria for implementing a capacity mechanism in deregulated electricity markets, in: Utilities Policy, Vol. 16, 184-193.
Barboza, D. (2003): Brokers Say Prudential Approved Trading, N.Y. Times, Nov. 8, at C1.
Baumol, W.J. (1959): Business Behavior, Value and Growth, New York.
Becker, G. (1968): Crime and Punishment: An Economic Approach, in: Journal of Political Economy, Vol. 76, 169-217.
Berle, A.A. and Means, G.C. (1933): The Modern Corporation and Private Property, New York.
Blair, M. and Stout, L. (1999): A team production theory of corporate law, in: Virginia Law Review, Vol. 85, 247-328.

Blair, M. and Stout, L. (2001a): Corporate accountability: Director accountability and the mediating role of the corporate board, in: Washington Law review, Vol. 79, 403-447.

Blair, M. and Stout, L. (2001b): Trust, trustworthiness, and the behavioural foundations of corporate law, in: University of Pennsylvania Law Review, Vol. 149, 1735-1810.

Boland, L. (2003): The Foundation of Economic Methodology: A Popperian Perspective, 2nd ed., London.

Boulding, K. (1969): Economics as a Moral Science, in: American Economic Review, Vol. 59, 1-12.

Brockner, J. (1992): The escalation of commitment to a failing course of action: Toward theoretical progress, in: Academy of Management Review, Vol. 17, 39-61.

Buechner, J. and Katzfey, J. (2006): Die Wirkung der Anreizregulierung in der Praxis, in: Zeitschrift fuer Energie, Markt, Wettbewerb, 6/2006, 44-47.

Burns, L.R. and Pauly, M.V. (2002): Integrated Delivery Networks: A Detour on the Road to Integrated Health Care?, in: Health Affairs, Vol. 21, 128-43.

Business Week (1979): A Dark Future for Utilities, May 28, 114.

Cebul, R.D., Rebitzer, J.B., Taylor, L.J. and Votruba, M. (2008): Organizational Fragmentation and Care Quality in the U.S. Health Care System, in: NBER Working Paper Series, No. 14212.

Christensen, M. and Knudsen, T. (2010): Design of Decision-Making Organizations, in: Management Science, Vol. 56, 71-89.

Chandler, A.D. (1962): Strategy and Structure: Chapters in the History of the American Industrial Enterprise, Cambridge, Mass.

Clegg, S.R. (1990): Modern Organizations: Organization Studies in the Postmodern World, London.

Coase, R.H. (1937): The Nature of the Firm, in: Economica, Vol. 4, 386-405.

Coglianese, C. (2007): Legitimacy and Corporate Governance, in: Delaware Journal of Corporate Law, Vol. 32, 159-167.

Cohen, K.J. and Cyert, R.M. (1975): Theory of the firm: resource allocation in a market economy, Englewood Cliffs.

CAIB (Columbia Accident Investigation Board) (2003): Volume 1, Washington D.C.

Cooter, R. and Ulen, Th. (2008): Law and Economics, 5th ed., Boston.

Cyert, R.M. (1988): The economic theory of organization and the firm, New York.

Cyert, R.M. and March, J.G. (1959): A behavioral theory of organizational objectives, in: Mason Haire (Ed.), *Modern Organization Theory*, New York, 76-90.

Cyert, R.M. and March, J.G. (1963): A Behavioral Theory of the Firm, Oxford.

Davis, G.F. and Marquis, C. (2005): Prospects for Organizational Theory in the Early 21st Century: Institutional Fields and Mechanisms, in: Organization Science, Vol. 16, 332-343.

Day, R. (1964): Review of Cyert and March, A Behavioral Theory of the Firm, in: Econometrica, Vol. 32, 461-65.

Day, R. and Sunder, S. (1996): Ideas and Work of Richard M. Cyert, in: Journal of Economic Behavior and Organization, Vol. 31, 139-148.

Demsetz, H. (1967): Toward a Theory of Property Rights, in: American Economic Review, Papers and Proceedings, Vol. 57, 347-359.

DiMaggio, P.J. and Anheier, H.K. (1990): A Sociological Conceptualization of Non-Profit Organizations and Sectors, in: Annual Review of Sociology, Vol. 16, 137-159.

DiMaggio, P.J. and Powell, W.W. (1983): The Iron Cage Revisited: Institutional Isomorphism and Collective Rationality in Organizational Fields, in: American Sociological Review, Vol. 48, 147-160.

DiMaggio, P.J. and Powell, W.W. (1991): Introduction, in: Powell, W.W. and DiMaggio, P.J. (Eds.), The New Institutionalism in Organizational Analysis, Chicago, 1-38.

Eisenhardt, K.M. (1985): Control: Organizational and economic approaches, in: Management Science, Vol. 31, 134-149.

Etzioni, A. (2009): The Capture Theory of Regulations – Revisited, in: Society, Vol. 46, 319-323.

Eurostat (2006): Gas and electricity market statistics, Data 1990-2006, Eurostat Luxembourg.

Fama, E.F. and Jensen, M.C. (1983): Separation of ownership and control, in: Journal of Law and Economics, Vol. 26, 301-325.

Faure, M. (2009): The Impact of Behavioural Law and Economics on Accident Law, Den Haag.

Felin, T. and Foss, N.J (2005): Strategic Organization: A Field in Search of Micro-Foundations, in: Strategic Organization, Vol. 3, 441-55.

Fischel D.R., Sykes A.O. (1996): Corporate crime, in: Journal of Legal Studies, Vol. 25, 319-349.

France, D. (2004): Our Fathers: The Secret Life of the Catholic Church in an Age of Scandal, New York.

French, J., and Raven, B.H. (1959): The bases of social power, in: Cartwright, D. (Ed.), Studies in social power, Ann Arbor, 150-167.

Frey, B.S. (2010): Superb Posner – but can we go further?, in: Journal of Institutional Economics, Vol. 6: 65-69.

Frey, B.S., Pommerehne, W.W. and Gygi, B.W. (1993): Economics, Indoctrination or Selection? Some Empirical Results, in: Journal of Economic Education, Vol. 24, 271-281.

Friedman, M. (1953): The Methodology of Positive Economics, in: Friedman, M. (Ed.), Essays in Positive Economics, Chicago, 3-43.

Furubotn, E.G. and Richter, R. (2005): Institutions and Economic Theory: The Contribution of the New Institutional Economics, 2nd ed., Ann Arbor.

Goerten, J., and Clement, E. (2006): Electricity prices for EU households and industrial consumers on 1 January 2006, in: Statistics in focus (Eurostat), No. 11.

Granovetter, M. (1985): Economic Action and Social Structure: The Problem of Embeddedness, in: American Journal of Sociology, Vol. 91, 481-510.

Greve, H.R. (1996): Patterns of competition: The diffusion of a market position in radio broadcasting, in: Administration Science Quarterly, Vol. 41, 29-60.

Grossman, S. and Hart, O. (1986): The Costs and Benefits of Ownership: A Theory of Vertical and Lateral Integration, in: Journal of Political Economy, Vol. 94, 691-719.

Groves, T. and Ledyard, J. (1987): Incentive Compatibility since 1972, in: Groves, T., Radner, R. and Reiter, R. (Eds.), Essays in Honor of Leonid Hurwicz. Minneapolis, 48-111.

Hall, C., Scott, C. and Hood, C. (2000): Telecommunications Regulation, London and New York.

Hart, O. and Moore, J. (1988): Incomplete Contracts and Renegotiation, in: Econometrica, Vol. 56, 755-785.

Haucap, J. and Just, T. (2010): Not Guilty? Another Look at the Nature and Nurture of Economics Students, in: European Journal of Law and Economics, Vol. 29, 239-254.

Hayek, F.A. (1989): The Pretence of Knowledge, in: American Economic Review, Vol. 79, 3-7.
Hayek, F.A. (2002): Competition as a Discovery Procedure, in: Quarterly Journal of Austrian Economics, Vol. 5, 9-23.
Heine, K. (2011): Inside the black box: Incentive regulation and incentive channeling on energy markets, in: Journal of Management and Governance (forthcoming).
Heine, K. and Kerber, W. (2002): European Corporate Laws, Regulatory Competition and Path Dependence, in: European Journal of Law and Economics, Vol. 13, 43-71.
Holmes, O.W. (1897): The Path of the Law, in: Harvard Law Review, Vol. 10, 457-478.

Jacobi, J.V. and Huberfeld, N. (2001): Quality Control, Enterprise Liability, and Disintermediation in Managed Care, in: Journal of Law, Medicine and Ethics, Vol. 29, 305-322.
Janulis, D.M. and Hornstein, A.D. (1985): Damned If You Do, Damned If You Don't: Hospitals' Liability for Physicians' Malpractice, in: Nebraska Law Review, Vol. 64 689-720.
Jensen, M.C. and Meckling, W.H. (1976): Theory of the firm: managerial behavior, agency costs and ownership structure, in: Journal of Financial Economics, Vol. 3, 305-360.
Johnson, V. (2007): What is Organizational Imprinting? Cultural Entrepreneurship in the Founding of the Paris Opera, in: American Journal of Sociology, Vol. 113, 97-127.
Jolls, C. (2007): Behavioural Law and Economics, in: Diamond, P. and Vartiainen, H. (Eds.), Economic Institutions and Behavioral Economics, Princeton, p. 115-155.
Jolls, C., Sunstein, C.R. and Thaler, R. (1998): A Behavioral Approach to Law and Economics, in: Stanford Law Review, Vol. 50, 1471-1550.
Joskow, P.L. (1991): The Role of Transaction Cost Economics in Antitrust and Public Utility Regulatory Policies, in: Journal of Law, Economics and Organization, Vol. 7, S53-S83.
Joskow, P.L. (2006): Incentive Regulation in Theory and Practice: Electricity Distribution and Transmission Networks, MIT Working Paper, January 21, 2006.

Kahneman, D., Slovic, P. and Tversky, A. (1982) (Eds.): Judgement under Uncertainty: Heuristics and Biases, Cambridge, Mass.

Kennedy, D. (1985): The Role of Law in Economic Thought: Essays on the Fetishism of Commodities, in: American University Law Review, Vol. 34, 939-1001.

Kerkmeester, H. (2003): A Note on the History of European Law and Economics: Wertheim's Dissertation, in: German Working Papers in Law and Economics: Vol. 2003, Paper 23.

Knittel, C.R. (2006): The Adoption of State Electricity Regulation: The Role of Interest Groups, in: Journal of Industrial Economics, Vol. 54, 201-222.

Koch, B.A. (2007): The "Principles of European Tort Law", in: ERA Forum, Vol. 8, 107-115.

Koh, W.T.H. (1992): Variable evaluation costs and the design of fallible hierarchies and polyarchies, in: Economics Letters, Vol. 38, 313-318.

Kole, S.R. and Lehn, K.M. (1997): Deregulation, the Evolution of Corporate Governance Structure and Survival, in: American Economic Review, Papers and Proceedings, Vol. 87, 421-425.

Kole, S.R. and Lehn, K.M. (1999): Deregulation and the Adaptation of Governance Structure: The Case of the U.S. Airline Industry, in: Journal of Financial Economics, Vol. 52, 79-117.

Korobkin, R.B. and Ulen, T.S. (2000): Law and Behavioural Science: Removing the Rationality Assumption from Law and Economics, in: California Law Review, Vol. 88, 1053-1146.

Koziol. H. (2006): Strict Liability in the New Austrian Draft on Liability Law, in: Koziol, H. and Steininger, B.C. (Eds.), European Tort Law 2004, Tort and Insurance Law Yearbook, Wien, 50-59.

Kraakman, R.H. (2009): Vicarious and corporate civil liability, in: Faure, M. (Ed.), Tort Law and Economics, Cheltenham, 134-149.

Krawiec K.D. (2000): Accounting for Greed: Unraveling the "Rogue Trader" Mystery, in: Oregon Law Review, Vol. 79, 301-338 (2000).

Krawiec K.D. (2003): Cosmetic Compliance and the Failure of Negotiated Governance, in: Washington University Law Quarterly, Vol. 81, 487-544.

Krawiec, K.D. (2005): Organizational Misconduct: Beyond the Principal-Agent Model, in: Florida State University Law Review, Vol. 32, 571-615.

Krawiec, K.D. (2009): The Return of the Rogue, in: Arizona Law Review, Vol. 51, 127-174.

Kreps, D.M. (1996): Corporate Culture and Economic Theory, in: Buckley, P.J. and Michie, J. (Eds.), Firms, Organizations and Contracts, Oxford, 221-275.

Kusserow, R.P. (1991): State Prohibitions on Hospital Employment of Physicians, Department of Health and Human Services, USA.

Laffont, J.-J. (1994): The New Economics of Regulation Ten Years After, in: Econometrica, Vol. 62, 507-537.

Lan, L.L. and Heracleous, L. (2010): Rethinking Agency Theory: The View from Law, in: Academy of Management Review, Vol. 35, 294-314.

Lazzarini, S.G., Miller, G.J., and Zenger, T.R. (2004): Order with some law: complementarity vs. substitution of formal and informal arrangements, in: Journal of Law, Economics and Organization, Vol. 20, 261-298.

Leibenstein, H. (1979): A Branch of Economics is Missing: Micro-Micro Theory, in: Journal of Economic Literature, Vol. 17, 477-502.

Léon, O.G. (1997): On the Death of SMART and the Birth of GRAPA, in: Organizational Behavior and Human Decision Processes, Vol. 71, 249-262.

Levinthal, D. (2005): Footnotes to the Behavioral Theory of the Firm, Wharton School, University of Pennsylvania, working paper.

Levitt, B. and March, J.G. (1988): Organizational Learning, in: Annual Review of Sociology, Vol. 14, 319-340.

Lewis, T.E. and Meade, R.B. (2007): Alternating Currents or Counter-Revolution? Contemporary Electricity Reform in New Zealand, Wellington.

Littlechild, S. (1983): Regulation of British Telecommunications Profitability, London, Department of Industry, HMSO.

Lobel, O. and Amir, O. (2008): Stumble, Predict, Nudge: How Behavioral Economics Informs Law and Policy, in: Columbia Law Review, Vol. 108, 2098-2138.

London, M. (2003). Antecedents and Consequences of Self-Verification: Implications for Individual and Group Development, in: Human Resource Development Review, Vol. 2, 273-293.

Love, I. (2010): Corporate Governance and Performance around the World: What We Know and What We Don't, in: World Bank Research Observer, Vol. 25, 1-29.

March, J.G. and Shapira, Z. (1987): Managerial perspectives on risk and risk taking, in: Management Science, Vol. 33, 1404-1418.

Marris, R.L. (1963): A Model of the Managerial Enterprise, in: Quarterly Journal of Economics, Vol. 77, 185-209.

McFadden, D. (2009): The human side of mechanism design: a tribute to Leo Hurwicz and Jean-Jacque Laffont, in: Review of Economic Design, Vol. 13, 77-100.

McClelland, D.C. (1961): The achieving society, Princeton.

McClelland, D.C. (1987): Human motivation, Cambridge, Mass.

Meyer, J. and Rowan, B. (1977): Institutionalized Organizations: Formal Structure as Myth and Ceremony, in: American Journal of Sociology, Vol. 83, 340-363.

Mikkelsen, A., Nybo, G., and Gronhaug, K. (2002): Exploring the impact of deregulation on HRM: the case of the Norwegian energy sector, in: International Journal of Human Resource Management, Vol. 13, 942-957.

Mitbestimmung (2006): Haben die Verbraucher Milliarden zu viel gezahlt?, in: Magazin Mitbestimmung, No. 07, 10-15.

Moore, J. (1992): The firm as a collection of assets, in: European Economic Review, Vol. 36, 493-507.

Mueller, D.C. (2004): Public Choice III, Cambridge, Mass.

Mueller, F. and Carter, C. (2007): 'We are all managers now': Managerialism and professional engineering in UK electricity utilities, in: Accounting, Organization and Society, Vol. 32, 181-195.

Narduzzo, A., and Warglien, M. (2008): Conducting Experimental Research on Organizational Routines, in: Becker, M.C. (Ed.), Handbook of Organizational Routines, Cheltenham, 301-324.

Nee, V. (2005): The New Institutionalism in Economics and Sociology, in: Smelser, N. and Swedberg, R. (Eds.), The Handbook of Economic Sociology, 2nd ed. Princeton, 49-74.

Nelson, R. and Winter, S. (1982): An Evolutionary Theory of Economic Change, Cambridge, Mass.

Nielsen, F. (2007): Economic Inequality, Pareto, and Sociology: The Route Not Taken, in: American Behavioral Scientist, Vol. 50, 619-638.

OFGEM (2008): Electricity Distribution Price Control Revenue Reporting: Regulatory Instructions and Guidance - Version 4, London.

Peltzman, S. (1976): Toward a More General Theory of Regulation, in: Journal of Law and Economics, Vol. 19, 211-240.

Pfeifenberger, J.P., and Tye, W.B. (1995): Handle with care. A primer on incentive regulation, in: Energy Policy, Vol. 23, 769-779.

Posner, R.A. (2010a): From the new institutional economics to organization economics: with applications to corporate governance, government agencies, and legal institutions, in: Journal of Institutional Economics, Vol. 6, 1-37.

Posner, R.A. (2010b): On the Receipt of the Ronald H. Coase Medal: Uncertainty, the Economic Crisis, and the Future of Law and Economics, in: American Law and Economics Review, Vol. 12, 265-279.

Projet Catala (2005): Avant-Projet de Reforme du Droit des Obligations (Articles 1101 à 1386 du Code civil) et du Droit de la Prescription (Articles 2234 à 2281 du Code civil); available at http://www.ladocumentationfrancaise.fr/rapports-publics/054000622/index.shtml.

Rajan, R.G. and Zingales, L. (1998): Power In A Theory Of The Firm, in: Quarterly Journal of Economics, Vol. 113, 387-432.

Rajan, R.G. and Zingales, L. (2000): The governance of the new enterprise, in: Vives, X. (Ed.), Corporate Governance, Cambridge, Mass, 201-226.

Rajan, R.G. and Zingales, L. (2001): The Firm As A Dedicated Hierarchy: A Theory Of The Origins And Growth Of Firms, in: Quarterly Journal of Economics, Vol. 116, 805-851.

Robertson, D.H. (1923): The control of industry, London.

Romano, R., (1985): Law as a Product: Some Pieces of the Incorporation Puzzle, in: Journal of Law, Economics and Organization, Vol. 1, 225-83.

Romano, R. (1993): The Genius of American Corporate Law, Washington.

Russo, M. (1992): Bureaucracy, Economic Regulation, and the Incentive Limits of the Firm, in: Strategic Management Journal, Vol. 13, 103-118.

Sah, R.K. (1991): Fallibility in Human Organizations and Political Systems, in: Journal of Economic Perspectives, Vol. 5, 67-88.

Sah, R.K. and Stiglitz, J.E. (1985): Human Fallibility and Economic Organization, in: American Economic Review, Papers & Proceedings, Vol.75, 292-297.

Sah, R.K. and Stiglitz, J.E. (1986): The Architecture of Economic Systems, in: *American Economic Review*, Vol. 76, 716-727.

Salancik, G. and Pfeffer, J. (1977): Who gets power: and how they hold on to it, in: Organizational Dynamics, Vol. 5, 3-21.

Santos, F.M. and Eisenhardt, K.M. (2005): Organizational Boundaries and Theories of Organization, in: Organization Science, Vol. 16, 491-508.

Scalia, A. (1989): The Rule of Law as a Law of Rules, in: University of Chicago Law Review, Vol. 56, 1175-88.

Schwartz, H. and Davis, S. (1981): Matching Corporate Culture and Business Strategy, in: Organizational Dynamics, Vol. 10, 30-48.

Shleifer, A. (1985): A Theory of Yardstick Competition, in: RAND Journal of Economics, Vol. 16, 319-327.

Silva, C., Wollenberg, B.F. and Zheng, C.Z. (2001): Application of mechanism design to electric power markets, in: IEEE Transactions on Power Systems, Vol. 16, 1-8.

Simester, D.I. and Wernerfelt, B. (2005): Determinants of Asset Ownership: A Study of the Carpentry Trade, in: The Review of Economics and Statistics, Vol. 87, 50-58.

Singh, A. (2003): Competition, Corporate Governance and Selection in Emerging Markets, in: Economic Journal, Vol. 113, F443-F464.

Sitkin, S.B. and Pablo, A.L. (1992): Reconceptualizing the Determinants of Risk Behaviour, in: Academy of Management Review, Vol. 17, 9-38.

Slovic, P. (2000) (Ed.): The Perception of Risk, London.

Smith, V.L. (2003): Constructivist and Ecological Rationality in Economics, in: American Economic Review, Vol. 93, 465-508.

Staw, B.M. (1976): Knee-deep in the Big Muddy: A study of escalating commitment to a chosen course of action, in: Organizational Behavior and Human Performance, Vol. 16, 27-44.

Stern, J. (1997): What makes an Independent Regulator Independent?, in: Business Strategy Review, Vol. 8, 67-74.

Stieglitz, N. and Heine, K. (2007): Innovations and the Role of Complementarities in a Strategic Theory of the Firm, in: Strategic Management Journal, Vol. 28, 1-15.

Stigler, G.J. (1971): The Theory of Economic Regulation, in: Bell Journal of Economics and Management Science, Vol. 3, 3-18.

Stinchcombe, A.L. (1965): Social structures and organizations, in: March, J.G. (Ed.), Handbook of Organizations, Chicago, 142-193.

Strang, D. and Soule, S.A. (1998): Diffusion in Organizations and Social Movements: From Hybrid Corn to Poison Pills, in: Annual Review of Sociology, Vol. 24, 265-290.

Sunstein, C.R. (2000) (Ed.): Behavioural Law and Economics, Cambridge, Mass.

Sykes, A.O. (1984): The economics of vicarious liability, in: Yale Law Journal, Vol. 93, 1231-1280.

Thaler, R.H. and Sunstein, C.R. (2008): Nudge. Improving Decisions about Health, Wealth and Happiness, New Haven.

Teece, D,J. (1996): Firm organization, industrial structure, and technological innovation, in: Journal of Economic Behavior & Organization, Vol. 31, 193-224.

Udehn, L. (2002): The changing face of methodological individualism, in: Annual Review of Sociology, Vol. 28, 479-507.

Van Boom, W.H. (2009): Inherent risk and organizational design in European tort law, in: Zeitschrift fuer Vergleichende Rechtswissenschaft, Vol. 108, 118-133.

Van Gennip, E.M.S.J. and Sillevis Smitt, P.A.E. (2000): The Netherlands Institute for accreditation of Hospitals, in: International Journal for Quality in Health Care, Vol. 12, 259-262.

Vanberg, V.J. (1992): Organizations as Constitutional Systems, in: Con stitutional Political Economy, Vol. 3, 223-253.

Verma, N. and Churchman, C.W. (1997): The Theory of the Firm: An Epistemological Analysis, in: Systems Practice, Vol. 10, 657-676.

Verma, K., Mitnick, B.M., and Marcus, A.A. (1999): Making Incentive Systems Work: Incentive Regulation in the Nuclear Power Industry, in: Journal of Public Administration Research and Theory, Vol. 9, 395-436.

Viscusi, W.K., Harrington, J.E., and Vernon, J.M. (2005): Economics of Regulation and Antitrust, 4th ed. Cambridge, Mass.

Vogelsang, I. (2002): Incentive Regulation and Competition in Public Utility markets: A 20-Year Perspective, in: Journal of Regulatory Economics, Vol. 22, 5-27.

Vromen, J.J. (1995): Evolution and efficiency: An inquiry into the foundations of 'new institutional economics', London.

Weick, K.E., Sutcliffe, K.M. and Obstfeld, D. (2005): Sensemaking and organizing. Organization Science, Vol. 16, 409-421.

West's Encyclopedia of American Law (2008): Vicarious Liability, 2nd. ed., Farmington Hills.

Willcox, A.W. (1960): Hospitals and the corporate practice of medicine, in: Cornell Law Quarterly, Vol. 45, 432-487.

Williamson, O.E. (1963): Managerial Discretion and Business Behavior, in: American Economic Review, Vol. 53, 1036-1057.

Williamson, O.E. (1975): Markets and hierarchies: analysis and antitrust implications, New York.

Williamson, O.E. (1985): The economic institutions of capitalism: firms, markets, relational contracting. New York.

Williamson, O.E. (1996): The Mechanisms of Governance, New York.

Williamson, O.E. (1998): Transaction Cost Economics: How it Works; Where it is Headed, in: De Economist, Vol. 146, 23-58.

Zenger, T.R., Lazzarini, S.G. and Poppo, L. (2002): Informal and formal organization in new institutional economics, in: Ingram, P. and Silverman, B.S. (Eds.), The New Institutionalism in Strategic Management, Amsterdam, 275-303.

Zingales, L. (2000): In Search of New Foundations, in: Journal of Finance, Vol. 55, 1623-1653.